HAS GOD GIVEN UP ON ME?

HAS GOD GIVEN UP ON ME?

DAVID EDWARDS

Building the New Generation of Believers

COOK COMMUNICATIONS MINISTRIES
Colorado Springs, Colorado • Paris, Ontario
KINGSWAY COMMUNICATIONS LTD
Eastbourne, England

NexGen® is an imprint of
Cook Communications Ministries, Colorado Springs, CO 80918
Cook Communications, Paris, Ontario
Kingsway Communications, Eastbourne, England

HAS GOD GIVEN UP ON ME?

First Printing, 2004
Printed in the United States of America
1 2 3 4 5 6 7 8 9 10 Printing/Year 08 07 06 05 04

Cataloging-in-Publication Data on file with the Library of Congress

ISBN 0781441420

*To **Flipopoly:** You've lived life with a godly passion and confidence that has enabled me to see the answers to life that never fail. I'm forever grateful.*

*To **Richard and Marilyn:** The heart holds the most important commitments in life. The friendship we share rises to the top of my heart. Thanks for being my committed friends and for helping me know how to answer the questions for life.*

CONTENTS

ACKNOWLEDGMENTS

I couldn't have written this book alone. Here are some of the people who helped make it happen.

Trey Bowden: Well, I guess I won't miss a chance to say thank you for your friendship and the great partnership in ministry. Most of all, for watering the rocks in my head.

Janet Lee: You had the vision and insight to set this project in motion. You believed in the value of these books and the impact they will have on thousands of people seeking answers to the questions of life.

Trevor Bron: You took my loaves and fishes and helped multiply them beyond my wildest dreams. A single book becomes a series. Thanks for blessing my life.

Bobby McGraw: I'm still struggling to find your breaking point. Full-time student, pastor—and you still had the time and energy to transcribe this entire project. Wouldn't have happened without you. Your work has been stellar.

Jim Lynch Everybody! You're my friend, my personal doctor who kept me alive—and you drove the comedy engine so well. Better peace through science. Thanks to Eric and Jim Hawkins, for the extra comedy fuel; it helped keep the engine going.

Gary Wilde: Thank you for your surgical editing skills. You preserved the integrity of the manuscripts, communicating the truths that needed to be told, while laughing at my jokes.

Shawn Mathenia: You finally got your very own line in one of my books. *This is it.* Thank you for your friendship and for looking out for me.

Ken Baugh and Frontline: Thank you for your continued passion that shows up in your ongoing work to reach a new generation. You guys are my home away from home.

The Sound Tracks: Train, Dave Matthews Band, Dave Koz, The Rippingtons, and Journey. Thanks for the inspiration.

The Questions for Life Series

I had just finished speaking at the White House and was eating lunch at Union Station with a young political consultant. We were halfway through our meal when I asked her, "What's life like for a postmodern inside the Beltway? You know, what kinds of questions do they ask?"

"They ask questions about the suffering and wrong in the world," she said, "about the church, and about who Jesus really is. You know, the questions that never fade."

Questions that never fade

Her label for those questions rose up inside of me, and this series of books flowed from that conversation. Postmoderns come wired with the need to answer the questions you'll find in these pages.

Most postmoderns have rejected the pat answers offered by today's spiritual leaders because they have found them to be inadequate for the daily life they face. They have seen others who accepted the ready-made answers but who still struggle making life work. They have no desire to repeat such mistakes. Instead, they challenge the real-life validity of the quick and easy answers.

The questions remain, but some of the questioners let their need for adequate answers diminish into the background. They give way to an apathy that says, "I've got more important things to do in my life than pursuing life's big questions." For others, finding resolution remains a priority. Yet even for them, life can become a never-ending "round-robin" of seeking solutions through new experiences.

Regardless of where you are at the moment, realize that the questions for life never truly fade away. They keep coming back, especially amidst your most trying times. They will keep knocking at your heart's door until you turn and acknowledge their crucial role in finding the life of your dreams. Until you take hold of real explanations, you'll remain constantly searching for the answers that never fail.

Answers that never fail

Spoken or unspoken, identified or unidentified, real answers are priceless. Until we find them, we're haunted by a lack of resolution in life. This unsettled life suffers constant turmoil and never-ending trouble. We look for direction that seems nonexistent, and this makes many of our decisions hard to live with. What price would we pay for a better way?

It's possible to spend a lifetime searching and never finding. Therefore, some would say that the reward comes not in the security of reaching the goal, but in the striving to obtain it. To these people I say: Why waste your life *looking* when you could be *living?*

The Creator of the universe holds the indelible answers we seek. They are not hidden, but they have often been obscured. They are veiled by some who place a higher value on *knowing* the answers than upon allowing the answers to change their lives. We need to push through and ask: What is the actual value of discovering answers that never fail? We'll find the value shining through in *what the answers produce in our lives*. When we discover these answers, our lives change in four supernatural ways. Finding them ...

Builds our outlook It's impossible to live a satisfying life without faith, meaning, and purpose. That's why each of us will place our faith in something or someone that is our primary value. We believe this person or thing will bring meaning and purpose to our life.

Without purpose, we'd have no reason to exist. So even the most cynical and withdrawn person seeks meaning in life. It may reside in something as mundane as keeping a pet iguana fat and happy. Or it could be that he finds meaning in something as twisted as making records and sleeping with young boys.

But life without an ultimate meaning and purpose becomes fragmented and chaotic. We roam from place to place, relationship to relationship, experience to experience, hoping to find something worth living for that endures. The iguana won't live forever. We also quickly discover that people fail us, that work is never-ending, that merely accumulating sensory experiences leads us down a continually darkening pathway.

There is no sense to life without meaning and purpose. There is no meaning and purpose without faith. And there is no faith until we answer the questions that never fade.

Brings ownership Discovering answers to the questions for life transforms us from merely being alive to actually having a life to live. We've all seen people who seem to just take up space in the world. They live for no apparent purpose. The things they do carry no meaning and make no appreciable impact on the people around them. They are alive, but they do not own a life.

> 66 Ownership of life begins when our head and our heart come together at a long-sought crossroads: where the questions that never fade meet the answers that never fail. 99

The questions for life can't be glibly answered, nor should they be made impotent through intellect. They must be answered in our hearts; they must settle down into the very center of our person. Ownership of life begins when our head and our heart come together at a long-sought crossroads: where the questions that never fade meet the answers that never fail.

Breaks us open Every question for life has a spiritual dimension. We may assume that answering the question of world hunger and suffering is only a physical matter, but that would be a wrong assumption. This question first finds its answer in a spiritual dimension, then the physical needs can be addressed in practical action. The same is true for all other questions for life; they each have a spiritual dimension.

The questions for life demand *powerful* answers that remain *present,* regardless of circumstance. The answers that never fade literally open us up to the things of God. That is, they lead us to find and apply his *power* and *presence* to the very heart of our question. These answers don't create despair; they settle disputes. They don't cause confusion; they construct a viable contract between life and us.

Brings an outworking Answering the questions for life develops an internal faith expressed in our observable behaviors. In other words, when we own the answers that never fail, our life takes on a meaning that others see and desire. This outworking of faith is extremely practical. It influences the choices we make, the words we speak, and the attitudes we reflect in daily life.

And this outworking can't help but grow a deep confidence within us. When never-failing solutions calm our internal struggles, we are able to move forward amidst seemingly insurmountable odds. We can work in an environment hostile to the things of Christ—and still live out our faith. We are confident that, although those around us may reject us, we are forever accepted by the One who matters most.

In these books, I have refused to "reheat" the old teachings. Instead of serving leftovers, I've dished up biblical answers that really do apply to the lives we live. These books keep it real, and I've written them with you in mind. I've used generous doses of humor and plenty of anecdotes (most of which actually happened to me).

I've made scant reference to other Christian authors, though, for a reason. In my attempt to make these books fresh, I chose to keep them uncluttered by the thoughts of others. Instead, I try to communicate God's thoughts from the Bible straight to your heart.

You'll notice that the title of each book forms a question. The titles of each chapter also appear as questions. But the content of each chapter *answers* that chapter's question. When read in their entirety, the chapters together answer the big question posed by each book.

You can read these books in any order; they each stand on their own in dealing with a single topic. At the end of each book you'll find questions that I hope will encourage an expanded discussion of the subject matter. Why not bring a group of friends together to talk things through?

Although this book series began over lunch inside the Beltway of Washington, D.C., I am aware that we are all bound together by the questions that never fade. As you read, I hope you will find the answers that never fail.

David Edwards
Summer, 2004

Introduction to
Has God Given Up on Me?

Y ou don't remember me, do you?"
I really don't like it when people ask me that,
because I usually *don't* remember them. I speak to thousands of people every year, in hundreds of locations. Over the past thirteen years, that's nearly half a million people in nearly twelve hundred different locations.

But I keep having those awkward moments. A guy walks up and expects me to remember him from a handshake several years before. I feel put on the spot; I don't want to be embarrassed, so I come up with extremely generic responses. Not long ago I was walking through a mall in Atlanta ...

"Hey, Dave Edwards! Is that *you?*"

"Why, yes, it is."

We shake hands and put on big, cheesy smiles. "Remember me? I attended your single's retreat a couple of years ago. We talked after the Saturday afternoon session. Remember?"

I looked up and to the right ... wracking my brain. "Yeah, you were there with a group of singles from your church."

"That's right!"

"And you had your study Bible with you."

"That's right! You have such a great memory. Do you remember Ray, the guy there with me?"

"Ray! How *is* Ray these days? We all sat there together and talked after lunch, didn't we?" ...

Something similar happens when we're confronted with the Bible and our knowledge of it—or our lack thereof. Sure, we remember. We talk in vague generalities or use acceptable catch phrases to communicate our understanding of Scripture.

"The Good Book says . ..."

"Money is the root of all evil."

"Abraham followed God and became the father of the Hebrew nation. Later in his life, he was elected president and shot in the head while attending a play in the Ford Theater."

When we pray, we try to sound as if we're genuinely "in touch" with the Almighty: "Our Father, Thou knowest full well that we Thy servants are truly endowed with Thy indwelling presence in the personhood of Thine only begotten Son in the form of Thy Holy Spirit who doth empower us to accomplish full well everything Thou settest before us this day."

I'm pretty sure words like those make King James proud—and leave God thoroughly confused.

Why has the Bible been so hard for us to grasp, understand, and remember? It remains the best-selling book of all time. It sits on shelves in more languages than any other book. It is more widely distributed and more readily available than Starbuck's coffee. It's so popular because it really does answer our biggest questions, especially the one we're asking in this book—about whether God has given up on us. In fact, throughout the Bible's pages we find God on a constant quest for us. Will we recognize him when he catches up to us at the mall ... or wherever?

If the Bible shows us how much the King of the Universe loves us, then we'll take great comfort and courage from its words. But if we can't understand the Bible, we lose out on all that comfort. Big problem! And the reason the Bible is so difficult for us to understand is *because of the way we read it.*

There's always an overhead projector in the churches where I speak. If I want, I can use thin, transparent sheets of plastic to write the points of my talk and project them

> **66 We use transparencies of presumption when we read the Bible. We bring our off-kilter ideas to the Scripture and lay them over it. 99**

behind me for all to see. Those transparencies serve as "overlays" to write on. In a similar way, we use transparencies of presumption when we read the Bible. We bring our off-kilter ideas to the Scripture and lay them over it, allowing our *presumptions* to determine our understanding of the Bible. Here are some things we wrongly assume:

That everything is being controlled Does the Bible really teach that all of life is governed by pre-set and invariable constants? No. But this kind of thinking effectively removes the drama from the relationship between God and humans. It replaces that relationship with predictable patterns of blessing and cursing, all based on a well-defined list of behaviors associated with each.

But God is not predictable, not a machine. He is surprising—and more than a little dangerous.

That the Bible is only personal Here's the idea that "my own experience of the Bible is enough." This presumptive overlay discounts what historical or denominational interpretations of Scripture can offer. It also tends to place the individual in a vacuum, determining for himself what the Bible means; the testimony and insights of others become irrelevant. Where, then, is the accountability to historically reliable biblical interpretation? Are we free to make the Bible mean anything we want it to mean, because it is such a *personal* book?

That this world is not my home This overlay of Scripture assumes that the real meanings of the Bible won't be discovered in the struggles of daily life. Instead, we'll only understand "by and by," in the utopia of God's future reign. Present-day struggles are distractions from our focus upon future glory with Jesus. Thus we approach the Bible only in the grandiose terms of heaven, hell, eternal rewards and eternal punishments, sheep and goats. This view of Scripture denies the reality that we live out our faith in a world that is very real, very messy, and very unpredictable.

These overlays—presumptions, assumptions, myths, false ideas—fog up our reading of the Bible. Perhaps we bring them to the text for fear we might lose our control of Scripture, that it might begin controlling us! When we risk removing all overlays and see the Scripture for what it truly is, one core truth emerges:

That we can be committed to the One who is committed to us This approach to reading the Bible is unlike the presumptive transparencies. It calls us to read the Bible for what it is, the Word of God. It invites us to commit to the Bible's Author. When we remove all the hindering overlays, the Bible does its real job: It simply reveals what a life of fidelity with God looks like.

We're going to survey that revelation and let ourselves remember the God who catches up with us in the middle of our busy lives. In the chapters to come, I've divided the books of the Bible into seven groupings to help you gain a sense of the entire biblical story. Each of the sections asks a single question that you put to God (and that God puts to you, as well). I haven't attempted to capture every story or to present the history or the context behind every book of the Bible, of course. Instead, I've tried to demonstrate *how the Scripture reveals the relationship between God and human beings.* These are seven classic divisions of the Bible viewed without traditional tactics and themes. The focus is the human/divine relationship. Each of the sections has a theme joined by a major question that is core to that part of the Scripture ...

Genesis—Deuteronomy: Liberate creation.
Question: "Do you know that I'm here?"

Joshua—Esther: Loyalty to commitment.
Question: "Will you trust me?"

Job—Ecclesiastes: Longing to connect.
Question: "Can you hear me?"

The Prophets: Looking toward change.
Question: "Do you see it?"

Matthew—John: Love comes.
Question: "Where is the love?"

The Epistles: Life continues.
Question: "What am I going to do with you?"

Revelation: Live courageously.
Question: "Have you forgotten me?"

In the sweep of Scripture, God goes out of his way to win people back to himself. He takes extreme measures to remain faithful in the midst of our unfaithful choices. The drama within God's move toward us comes through in the freedom of choice he's provided. He always says "yes," but we have the option of saying "no."

In the garden on the night before Jesus was arrested, tried, and crucified, he too had freedom—the same freedom to choose whether or not he would carry out God's will to its ultimate end, the cross. Thankfully, he chose to complete his assignment. Yet while on the cross, Jesus expressed the same feelings of abandonment that we have often felt: "My God, My God, why have you forsaken me?" The irony of Scripture is that this One had eternally co-existed in equality with the Father of heaven. Nevertheless, he cried out with the question we have all asked of God: "Have you given up on me?"

Chapter One

WHAT'S THE DEAL WITH THE BIBLE?

People today don't understand the Bible. I know the signs. *You really don't know the Bible if ...*

- you think "concordance" is a type of china dinnerware;
- you think having a leather-bound Bible makes you more spiritual (and that writing in it makes God mad at you);
- you heard about the *New* Testament and asked, "When is it coming out?"—because you really like sequels;
- you think the minor prophets were all under twenty-one;
- you believe *apostle, apostasy,* and *apocrypha* all mean the same thing;
- you think the Gideons wrote some of the Bible;
- you think part of the resurrection story includes Jesus coming out of the tomb and seeing his shadow;
- you think "Passover" is a football term;

- you've tried to find your street on the maps in the back;
- you need a thumb-indexed Bible to find the Book of Genesis;
- you think it's part of the "Left Behind" series;
- you've read only three parts: your name, who gave it to you, and the verse that says, "Wives, submit to your husbands";
- your favorite verse is: "God helps those who help themselves."

So what's the deal with the Bible? It's more than a collection of stories. And it's much more than a history of the Hebrew's interactions with God. It supercedes the characterization of wisdom literature, and it bypasses the label of children's stories.

Of course, we might know what the Bible *isn't*. But we'll still need to get a handle on the basic nature, purpose, and scope of the Bible to see what it *is*. We can start by viewing it in five distinct, yet unified, ways.

> **"**Imagination keeps the Bible fresh so we can view it as more than a boring recitation of the 'good old days.'**"**

It's the memory of God's future acts

This is more than a history, more than a chronology of events. The Bible captures the drama between the Creator of the universe and the people of his creation. Before the written

Scriptures ever existed, the stories of the Bible were verbally passed from one person to another, from one generation to the next. The memories of God's activities came through in the stories parents told as they tucked their children into bed for the night, while they ate breakfast together before school, and while they worked together making the family's liveli-hood. The integrity of these stories was carefully guarded, and the accuracy maintained through the years is impressive.

The purpose of sharing these stories was to preserve the knowledge of God's *past* activities and keep it alive in the present. The stories also helped bolster the hearers' faith that God would be available in their *future* difficult times.

These stories were told so often and so accurately that people constantly had them in mind. This gave them power to trust God in almost any circumstance. The stories helped them know that God was hardly remote, distant, or abstract, nor was he a self-serving tyrant. He was lovingly present.

The people recited the acts of God and made claims about his character that they truly believed. These confessions were their own, not their parents. They could see how God's activ-ities on the earth shaped human history. They could docu-ment how he had brought freedom from oppression, the capacity for life in the midst of helplessness, and the promise of a hopeful future.

Just as today's stories bring to life the imagination, these true accounts of God's actions brought history and substance to the imaginations of the hearers. After all, just hearing facts of history without imagination tends to make history dry and dull. Similarly, imagination keeps the biblical past from becoming stuck there, from being one dimensional, dull, and closed. Imagination keeps the Bible fresh so we can view it as more than a boring recitation of the "good old days."

I'm simply saying there's a different way to read your Bible than what you may be used to. Why just read for the facts when you can read for the drama pulsing within real-life relationships? Why not capture the picture behind the picture, the drama underlying the plot of the whole story?

Let's go beyond the attempts to somehow grasp THE MEANING of Scripture and see it for what it is: the recorded drama of God's interactions with his creation. This is not to say that the Bible is the drama in its entirety; it continues through the lives of all believers. The Bible is living and active, and it keeps impacting our attitudes, our faith, our whole lives.

It's the mystery of God's greatness

The Bible also conveys the fullest demonstration of just how great God is. There is mystery in the Bible's stories, just as there is mystery inherent in the greatness of God. If we could quickly comprehend the extent of divine greatness, it would cease to hold wonder for us. If there were no wonder, then God could be contained. And that container would at once become greater than God.

God is both distant and near at the same time. He exceeds our physical abilities to see, feel, and touch. But he is, at the same time, Immanuel, "God with us." He is in all places at the same time and yet ever-present with us in the smallest recesses of our hearts. He is all-knowing, yet waits for us to tell him what's on our minds. The mystery of God is that he is all of these things at the same time; however, the sum of them does not make up God. He is greater than any and all of the things we think he is. Our minds are finite; he is infinite. Therefore, our theologies always fall short of his reality.

> **He is greater than any and all of the things we think he is. Our minds are finite; he is infinite.**

God promises to be with us, evidence of the value he places on our relationship with him. We relate to a living, active, caring, intervening God. He is intimately interested in the things that interest us. He invites the relationship and always stands ready to embrace us when at last we say "yes."

God is our refuge and our strength, the always-present help when we face trouble. For too long we've seen God as the static, unreachable deity in heaven. He is not a passive object that we must adore and revere from afar. Instead, the God of the Bible laid aside his eternal nature and replaced it with the temporary nature of a man, Jesus. This transformation is the only way we could ever have grasped the mysterious truth that a personal relationship with God is available. And God is more than simply *with* us, he is *for* us.

It was made under guidance

The Bible *is* the Word of God. This is different from saying that it merely *contains* the Word of God (as the *Reader's Digest* contains articles). The Bible is God's written document that reveals to us who he is, in word and deed.

The Bible says about itself that it was "inspired," according to 2 Timothy 3:16. We could translate the Greek word in that verse, *theopneustos,* as: "God-breathed." Some have understood this to mean that God dictated the Scripture, word for word, in a mechanical way. Others understand this term to mean that the human authors of the Scripture were carried along in a strength not of their own, and empowered with supernatural wisdom and abilities, so that the very words and thoughts of God could be captured in written form. In this view, the authors' personalities and writing styles would still come through. (This is indeed the case. The Greek of fisherman Peter, in style and vocabulary, is much different from Doctor Luke's!)

In any case, the facts surrounding this remarkable book make the cohesive story line an even greater miracle. The sixty-six Bible books were written by over forty different authors from all walks of life: shepherds, farmers, tent-makers, physicians, fishermen, priests, philosophers, and kings. These authors wrote the books of the Bible during a period of fifteen hundred years. They used three different languages: Aramaic, Hebrew, and Greek. All this time and variety! Nevertheless, the themes and plots unfold, step by step, in the story of human redemption. How could this book have come together without supernatural guidance?

The Bible we have today is said to be "canonized." The term *canon* comes from the Greek word for "measuring rod." In other words, during the early centuries of the church the Bible's books came to be recognized as inspired. That is, no one suddenly decided this was so; it was obvious to all the church leaders, a recognition by consensus, of a fact of reality. Early councils confirmed that these sixty-six books met the measure, or standard, of divine inspiration and authority from the beginning. (Certain other Christian books around at the time were good for devotional reading or information, but they didn't meet the measure. It's the same today.) So these sixty-six became the collection of writings accepted by the apostles and the leadership of the early Christian church. They continue today as our Bible, the basis for Christian belief and activity.

It's the means of our growth

The Bible realistically shows what humans are capable of accomplishing by willpower alone. When we get enmeshed in habits and tied to vested interests, we lack the ability to change ourselves regardless of how badly we want to. This comes through in the Old Testament account of Israel's history as the people moved toward exile in Babylon. The poets who wrote to warn Israel of her sin realized that she was incapable of letting go of it and choosing God's plan for them. If they were to have newness, they must have another source for change. Therefore, the Lord said: "I will give you a new heart and put a new spirit within you; and I will remove the heart of stone … and give you a heart of flesh" (Ezek. 36:26). This verse describes God as ready to take radical steps in order to give Israel new organs of decision-making to replace the old ones. They had become incapable of making correct decisions.

In Ezekiel 20, God admits to himself, and on behalf of Israel, that they are incapable of change. Therefore, God

> ❝ There is no more radical idea than this in the Bible: God repents. ❞

makes a new covenant. This is an agreement that depends not on the turning of Israel, but on a new possibility worked out by God. It makes change possible because God himself empowers it. When there is ongoing dysfunction between God and his people, and the fracture is unavoidable, when Israel was called to repent and could not, the Lord himself repents.

There is no more radical idea than this in the Bible: God repents. Here God is not presented primarily as all-knowing, all-powerful, or all-present. Instead, he is presented as the covenant partner who freely intervenes with a fresh decision toward the covenant partner. In this role, God is not a motionless object. Quite the contrary. He is a dynamic, responding covenant partner who, in faithful compassion, acts in various ways to renew, restore, and transform our relationship with him.

The striking announcement of the Bible is that God has willingly limited himself to come into covenant with stubborn people. He changes his plans in order that we might understand his Word. Because of his commitment to humankind, God withdraws deserved punishment upon the people he loves.

This thought suggests to us that he will not fit any predictable religious ideas. God is free to act according to his perfect purposes and not according to any pre-designed regulation we might apply to him. The Lord is unlike any other god in the world, whether that be ancient or modern. The Lord wills covenant and he insists that people turn to him. He asks nothing of them that he himself is unwilling to do. God is radically pro-people. It is his turning that makes it possible for us to turn to him.

This ability of God to turn and to change (i.e., decide to withhold judgment) brings to bear some striking new thoughts regarding our own identity. In his infinite maturity, God changes his plans. We are created in his divine image. As such, we find our most mature humanity wrapped up in our ability to ask forgiveness, in our ability to care so intensely and to change so liberally that we can actually make vows and keep them. In this way, we are most like the One who seeks covenant with us.

It's the message to every generation

I'm going to capitalize the word *Message* in this section to remind you that the Bible's essential proclamation is much more than a nice set of ideas or rules to live by. It is a word of eternal salvation. The Message of the Bible is never-ending, and it never returns empty. It always impacts the lives of those it touches. The Bible is God's Message to every generation, calling persons into relationship with God.

We can't define this relationship by scientific or logical terms. It cannot be measured, quantified, or tested under laboratory conditions. It cannot be duplicated, transferred, or transplanted from one life to another. It is distinctly individual and personal; people must experience it for themselves.

The Message of the Bible calls us out of selfishness and the pursuit of success for the sake of success. Both of these lead to emptiness rather than fullness. It pushes us onward toward a more radical view of God than we have ever had before. No longer do we see him removed and unreachable; now he is nearby and in active relationship with us. We are moved by his presence, and he is moved by our heart of movement toward him in our actions, attitudes, and choices.

> **The reason many people click off from the church, the Bible, and Christianity is they have never seen anyone living authentically in covenant with God.**

The Bible's Message challenges us in our everyday living. No longer is ordinary life acceptable. The full life initiated and seeded into our lives by the covenant love of God is the only acceptable life for the believer. It is an individual journey of faith toward becoming more like Christ.

The Message of the Bible opens us up to the real life of God, the life that is dramatic, dynamic, and drenched in the very substance of existence each of us seeks. The reason many people click off from the church, the Bible, and Christianity is they have never seen anyone living authentically in covenant with God. They don't know what real life looks like. They believe that what they have seen in the lives of other Christians is not life, but slavery to a pre-determined set of ideals. They misunderstand the relationship with God as a static, boring life, with no variety or spontaneity. In truth, this life overflows with drama and the adventure of the unknown.

The Message of the Bible is that the One who loves us seeks us with all his heart. We are the object of his desire. We are what his heart beats for. The Bible immerses us in this infinite love story.

DO YOU KNOW I'M HERE?

E verywhere I go I find people who want to talk about the Bible heroes. They usually point out how much better than us those spiritual champions were. In fact, however, many of them had some real problems. Suppose we applied current psycho-babble terms to some of their behaviors? I mean, if we were to categorize their mental disorders, they'd look like the "Who's Who" of Psych Central! Think about it ...

- Adam and Eve were co-dependent enablers who fed each other's desire to fulfill their own wills.
- Noah showed signs of acute antlophobia (the fear of floods).
- Moses struggled with trichotillomania (constantly pulling out one's hair).
- Isaac must have suffered PTSD (Post-Traumatic Stress Disorder) after he was almost offered as the sacrifice *du jour* by his father, Abraham.
- Jacob would have been diagnosed with ODD (Oppositional Defiant Disorder), manifested by a

pattern of negativism, hostility, and refusing to comply with family rules.

- Joseph had a grandiose sense of self-importance and was preoccupied with fantasies of unlimited success and power. Did he have Narcissistic Personality Disorder?
- Ruth surely had separation anxiety and would not leave Naomi, but instead said, "Wherever you go, I will go."
- Lot's wife had OCD—Obsessive Compulsive Disorder—because she just couldn't stop turning around to look behind her.
- Jonah suffered Avoidant Personality Disorder, manifested in his willingness to face the ocean depths rather than interact with the citizens of Nineveh.

Hey, everyone needs help. All of these Bible heroes needed God's help, and so do each of us. Just because we need God's help doesn't mean that we have failed in some way. Most of the time, even these Bible heroes needed more of God's help than they accepted or asked for.

Throughout the first five books of the Bible, the question, "Do you know I'm here?" is raised from both God and human beings. In each of the first five books, God asks the question of the people as he pursues them to join him in the full drama of relationship. The people also cry out to God through this question, "God, do you see what we endure every day? Do you know that I'm here?" In all five of the first books of the Bible, God is the first to reach out with the answer mankind is crying out to hear. "I am here, available and ready to provide whatever you need. Do you know that I'm here?" We'll focus on the way this question takes shape in each of these five books.

Genesis: Life is made available

In the very first chapter of Genesis, God demonstrated that he is the life-giver by ... creating life. He then set about the task of liberating individual parts of the cosmos in order so they could fulfill specific purposes: light to illumine the cosmos; water to feed plant life and to serve as the domain for water creatures; land to provide the foundation for the rest of life; air for animals and humans to breathe. Each part of the creation fulfilled its own unique function, and together it all made up the cosmos. Creation became the first evidence that God is the life-giver, the source of all life.

Not long after God placed Adam and Eve in the Garden of Eden, they willfully chose to pursue their own agenda, a choice that placed them in bondage and put them in need of liberation. That same day God came for his walk with them. But when they heard him coming, they hid themselves in the bushes. They realized that they were naked, and they were embarrassed.

God knew they were hiding but called out to them anyway, "I'm here. Where are you?" Adam called out from behind the bush, "I'm here, but I'm embarrassed to come out and greet you, because I'm naked." God provided the remedy they needed and covered their sin. Even though they were forced to leave the garden, God allowed them to keep the life he had given them, albeit with changes. God also bailed out plenty of other people in this first book of the Bible:

- Noah needed saving from a watery judgment of the earth. God directed him to build a boat large enough to house his entire family and two of every kind of animal from the face of the earth.
- Abraham had received a promise from God that he'd become the father of a great nation. But he was nearly 90 years old—and still no kid. Guess what happened then.
- Jacob was a "screw-up" type of guy and often needed God to bail him out of his mistakes. But late in his life he willingly received the deliverance God had prepared for him.
- Joseph often needed a deliverer and helper: He got thrown in a well, then thrown into prison, then thrown into national leadership. God had taken Joseph from the pit to the prison and from the prison to the king's courts in order to preserve the lives of his brothers and his father.

The message of Genesis is that life has been made available for everyone. The Creator is, and always will be, the protector and provider for all his creatures. He consistently calls out to his creation, "I'm here, come to me, and you will find the life you seek."

Exodus: Empires are cancelled

In this book, God continues to say, "I'm here with you." He calls his people to walk away from their slavery into the unknown that he holds in his hand. Mighty Moses was the one to lead them.

Following a few unsuccessful meetings with Pharaoh, along with several very unpleasant plagues—including flies, frogs, blood, darkness, and locusts—Moses told all the people to get ready; they'd be leaving the next day. He also instructed them to stay indoors all night. But before they retired, they were to cover their doorframes with the blood of a lamb. That night the death angel would visit, and he would *pass over* every house with the required blood on it. (Hence, the celebration of Passover to this day.)

By painting their doors with the blood, the people were acknowledging God's presence in their tough situation. They were reminding God that they were present, too, ready to cooperate with his plan. This could have been confusing, though. I can just hear a young Hebrew man discussing with his elderly, hard-of-hearing neighbor:

"Moses said the blood of a lamb," the young man says.

"You know, son, I've been around this place a lot longer than you have. And I know what I heard. Moses for sure said, 'the butt of a ram'."

"Yeah, well, who knows from painting doorposts, anyway? Blood of a lamb, butt of a ram—what could go wrong?"

> "Who knows from painting doorposts, anyway? Blood of a lamb, butt of a ram—what could go wrong?"

Later that night, every blood-painted door throughout Egypt was spared a visit from the death angel. But those families who hadn't followed Moses' instructions received their visit and lost the first-born of the household. The next morning, Moses led all the people out of Egypt.

But Pharaoh and his army were soon chasing them. Behind them were the approaching chariots, in front of them was the Red Sea. Moses prayed, "God, do you know we're here in this dangerous situation?"

"I know you are there," God responded. "But do you and the people know that I am here, and I will provide everything you need to face this situation?" God told Moses to stretch out his rod over the water, and he would divide it so the people could cross and avoid the wrath of Pharaoh.

Right before their eyes, God destroyed the very thing that had held them bondage. This is perhaps the time God asks this question the loudest, *"Do you know that I'm here?"*

Each of us has our own personal empire—places, people, or powers—that hold us in bondage. In the same way that God cancelled the empire of bondage for the Hebrews, he can, does, and will, cancel the places, people, or powers, that enslave us.

Leviticus: Fugitives are found

For over four hundred years the Hebrews had been slaves. After they escaped Egypt, during their wanderings in the wilderness, God led them by clouds during the daylight hours and by a pillar of fire at night. Every step of the way God's leadership was evident in these physical manifestations. In every step they took, they could *see* God's question: "Don't you know that I'm with you all the way?"

We are like the Hebrew people, somehow we miss the most obvious indications that God is aware and present—

even when he's clearly visible every step of the way. He delivered us from bondage, but we continue to return to live in the bondage rather than live in the freedom he provides.

In many of the places I speak, I know there are young adults who attend only to return to the enslavements God has already freed them from in the past. They remain in debilitating relationships, continue to practice self-destructive habits, and hold onto demoralizing attitudes. The same God who delivered the Hebrews from Egyptian slavery, has delivered them. And like the Hebrews, they still find the familiarity of bondage comfortable.

The Hebrew people needed to know that God was still with them, and God still wanted the people to know that their relationship with him was everything they needed. In relationship with him, he would show them how to handle all their interpersonal relationships, how to make special days reflect that never-ending relationship, and how to maximize their witness in the world. The key theme of the Book of Leviticus appears in verse 20:26, "You are to be holy to Me, for I the LORD am holy; and I have set you apart from the peoples to be Mine."

But how would they learn holiness? Coming out of over four hundred years of slavery, the Hebrew people had no regular methods to affirm their corporate connection with God. In Leviticus, God detailed several festivals and feasts that would help. One of these was the annual atonement and scapegoat.

In this "connection ceremony," the high priest would demonstrate God's forgiveness for the people. After the offering of animal sacrifices, the final part of the ceremony involved the priest laying his hands on the head of a goat.

> **Feel the relief and freedom as you watch the scapegoat carrying your sins out into the wilderness where they would never again be found.**

He was, in effect, laying the sins of the people on that goat. Then the goat was released into the wilderness, carrying away the sins of the people.

Imagine the power of this event as if you were one of the Hebrew fugitives. Feel the relief and freedom as you watch the scapegoat carrying your sins out into the wilderness where they would never again be found. Sense the gratitude toward God; he had provided a way for you to draw near to him.

For too long the people had cried out to God, "Do you know that we are here?" Now God had established regular times of worship that reinforced his abiding presence with them. He also provided a way for them to openly communicate their needs.

The purpose behind God's rescue of the people out of slavery was to establish them as a people for himself. They were to model his passion for the redemption of creation through their conduct and their connection with him. Their ultimate contribution would be to fully cooperate with his plan of cosmic redemption.

Our contribution is the same. We are to live in such a way with God and our fellow humans that the rest of the world sees what a difference it makes to have an intimate relationship with God. The seemingly endless lists of rules in Leviticus shows us that decisions we make directly impact others. As believers, we do not live in a bubble; instead, we live among people watching to see whether God truly is there … within us.

> **As believers, we do not live in a bubble; instead, we live among people watching to see whether God truly is there … within us.**

The whole point of Leviticus is: God calls us to connect with him, to connect with each other, and to connect with the world. We are to do so in a way that shows we're convinced God is there for us. Leviticus helps fugitives of every age live in authentic enjoyment of God. That authenticity will come through in the way we worship, work with others, and welcome other fugitives into a heavenly freedom.

Numbers: A future and a hope are present

In the Book of Numbers, God calls his people to take possession of the inheritance he provided for them. Their inheritance was more than the physical land that lay before them. It included the complete possession of their identity in God. Everything they had experienced in their deliverance from Egypt and their trek through the wilderness had brought them to the point of seeing God as he truly is—and to seeing themselves as they truly were. God is the *giver* of the inheritance; they are the intended *possessors*.

God had consistently called out to the people, "I have a future and a hope for you. If you seek me, you will find them both." The people had cried out long and hard for an identity, a hope, and a future. In Numbers, the people must decide whether or not they will trust in the Giver.

One of the central passages of this book is chapter 13. Moses sent out twelve spies to investigate the land God had promised them. After traveling the land and discovering everything it had to offer, the spies returned to the camp and gave their report: ten negative accounts and only two positive ones. The ten pessimistic reports read like the review of a B movie (when it was really a film that ought to capture eleven Academy awards). The two positive reports—about a wonderful land flowing with milk and honey—were so overwhelmed by the other ten that they carried no weight with the people. Instead of believing the giver of the inheritance, the people sided with ten fearful men.

Why were those guys afraid? Because the inhabitants

> **The ten pessimistic reports read like the review of a bad B movie (when it was really a film that ought to capture eleven academy awards).**

were tall, so large that "we were like grasshoppers in our own eyes." The words of the two other spies echoed God's offer of possession, but the people had already decided against fighting with supposed giants. In reality, they had chosen to reject God's inheritance for them.

In 14:20–24, God judged the people by forbidding any of that generation ever to set foot inside the land of inheritance. Instead, they wandered in the wilderness

> " God's promises are often closer than we realize. But we never obtain them without some sort of struggle. "

until the entire generation of infidelity died. Then God raised up for himself a new generation of people who saw themselves as he saw them: possessors of the inheritance. It took forty years, and during that time God fed the people, clothed them, and taught the new generation the importance of a daily trust in him. For these forty years God continuously asked the people, "Do you know I'm here? I've always *been* here, and I will always *be* here!"

Eventually the new generation pushed into the land asking God, "Do you see that we are here, taking possession of our inheritance?" God's promises are often closer than we realize. But we never obtain them without some sort of struggle.

God provides a future and a hope for us all. It resides where his identity and ours meet. Before we can ever possess the inheritance, the inheritance must possess us.

Deuteronomy: Relationships are revolutionized

Just before the people went in to possess the land, they paused in Moab. There Moses delivered a lengthy discourse, which is our Book of Deuteronomy. In this presentation, he refreshed the memory of God's faithfulness to the people of Israel. Moses presented its content all at once, as the people camped by the Jordan River waiting for their marching orders to advance. This book shows a clear transition between the wilderness wanderings and the possession of the Promised Land.

Moses' speech has four parts. The first two points remind us that God always stands asking the question, "Do you know that I'm here?" The third and fourth points represent both the nation and God asking each other the eternal accountability question, "Do you know that we are one together?"

Are you standing on the brink of your own inheritance these days? Will you move ahead in faith?

All of us enter times in our lives when we stand gazing at the brightest future and the deepest hope we can possibly know. At these times we must reorient ourselves back into our identity with God. Our possession of the future and the hope depends on this reorientation.

We must not only agree with all these truths *about* God, we must also unconditionally choose *him*. Whenever we completely accept him, we are also completely accepting his resolve. It is impossible to ever separate God from his purposes.

Throughout the first five books of the Bible, God consistently raises one question: "Do you know that I'm here?"

Regardless of how bad situations appear, God is always there, and we are never left alone. At the same time, the God who lovingly pursues us is big enough to let us ask the same question of him: "Do you know that *I'm* here, Lord?"

The question brings health to relationships. It inevitably leads the two parties toward each other, if they are committed to reaching each other in love. God has made this commitment toward us. Before we move on in our study of the Bible, wouldn't it be appropriate for us to take some time to meet with God at our own place of rest? Regular reminders like these in Deuteronomy will strengthen the faith of us all. And faith is the key to moving on in our understanding of Scripture.

Chapter Three

WILL YOU TRUST ME?

Our world is filled with self-improvement books, tapes, and courses. One of the most popular courses offers memory improvement. It promises name recall as we associate the sound of someone's name with a noticeable feature on his face or in his personality. I never took the course, but a friend of mine did. He taught me one or two of the techniques, which I applied on one of my church-speaking trips. Recently, when I returned to that church, I couldn't actually remember the pastor's name—but I *did* remember that he had a small fragment broken out of his glasses, and he had really bad breath. Wait! ... Was it ... Chip ... Hallitos?

We're always looking for improvements in ourselves. Maybe it's because we so desperately need them.

The Hebrew nation also needed to make improvements, and they tried many different ways to accomplish what they thought was in their best interest. But God sent enforcers, called "judges," to continually call the people back to the correct way. The judges' constant reminder to the people was that God was faithful and would always lead them in the right way. He was, and is, worthy of our trust.

The theme of trust between God and people binds together this collection of books (Joshua through Esther). Let's look closer:

Joshua: Trust God when facing the unknown

The Book of Joshua opens in the middle of one of Joshua's private moments with God. No one else is around. He sees the daunting task awaiting him, and Joshua fears he may not be up to it. God comes to Joshua at this moment of decision to reinforce in his mind that he is the man of the hour. He is chosen to carry out the super-sized task of Promised Land invasion.

Confident beginnings "Moses My servant is dead; now therefore arise, cross this Jordan, you and all this people, to the land which I am giving to them, to the sons of Israel" (Josh. 1:2).

The time had come for a change. For at least the past forty years, Joshua had followed Moses' commands, but now God told Joshua he would be responsible for speaking God's words to the people. Underlying everything God said to Joshua was the question, "Will you trust me? If you will then don't let this book of the law leave your mouth; instead, meditate on it day and night so that your way will be directed and you will have guaranteed success."

The only direction Joshua had known was Moses' as he followed God's leadership. But now he would be pointing the way for the people. Again God asked, "Will you trust me? If you do, every place you walk I will deliver into your hands. I will lead you and the people into the full inheritance I'm giving to them ... *if* you will trust me." God was beginning a new work in the lives of Joshua and the people. They would both soon learn just how quickly and decisively God acts.

Tactical progress "Pass through the midst of the camp and command the people, saying, 'Prepare provisions for yourselves, for within three days you are to cross this Jordan, to go in to possess the land'" (Josh. 1:11).

Three days after Joshua met with God, he led the people of Israel across the Jordan River. This mass of people camped near Jericho, waiting to take the city. Then one morning Joshua told them how it would happen: They would walk around the city in silence, once each day for six days, and then seven times on the seventh day. On the seventh day the priests would blow their trumpets, and the people would shout. That's when God would bring the walls crashing down.

The plan sounded as foolish to the people as it does to us. Except we know it worked. God's purpose in the plan was to deepen Israel's trust in him. He could have had them lay siege to the city, of course. Instead, he gave them a plan that required total faith.

Ever feel the same about some of God's ways with you? More often than not, we mistake no visible action with a lack of effectiveness on God's part. Our problems are real and weigh heavily on

> 66 More often than not, we mistake no visible action with a lack of effectiveness on God's part. 99

our minds. When we see no visible activity from God, we tend to think that he's forgotten about our scary circumstances. The problem is perspective. We're looking for exterior changes when, most of the time, God is working on the situation from the inside out. He seeks to grow our faith as he did with his people at Jericho.

In the final chapter of Joshua, the great leader tells the people to put away their idols and serve only their Lord God. Trust in his promises, trust in his abilities to uphold his promises, and trust in his character not to violate or break his promises. Trust is the elemental ingredient of the covenant between us and God.

> 66 **This man's relationship with the true God had degenerated into a superstition.** 99

Judges: Trust God when tempted to drift

> *In those days there was no king in Israel; everyone did what was right in his own eyes.*
>
> —Judges 21:25

This statement summarizes the core struggle of the entire Book of Judges. It is the source of the peoples' problems and the reason they needed the judges.

Religion is reduced to superstition Judges 17 dramatically demonstrates what happens when people simply do what is "right in their own eyes." Micah (not the prophet) filled his house with many different idols. He apparently wanted to cover all his spiritual bases and warrant the fullest measure of every god's blessing, including Jehovah God. So he invited a true priest to come and live with him to serve as his own, private religious practitioner before Jehovah.

Obviously, his idol worship violated the most basic Hebrew teachings. Yet, because Micah had decided for himself what was right and wrong, he found it easy to employ the services of a live-in priest. This man's relationship with the true God had degenerated into a superstition. He housed idols; he also housed God's representative—just to cover his religious bases!

Today many people attempt to accomplish the same thing by being good in the hopes of winning God's approval. They pay homage to the gods of their own choosing, though: the moral codes they've chosen to make "sacred" for themselves. Yet they have no genuine relationship with any of their gods. *They have traded sincerity for superstition.*

The rule of God is relinquished for security Judges 18 reveals how the tribe of Dan chose not to inherit the land assigned to them; instead, they wanted a different territory. Strong people occupied their assigned land, a people who could only be driven out by force. The Danites surveyed the situation and chose another territory occupied by a peaceful people with weak defenses. They also kidnapped Micah's private-duty priest to be their own priest! With the prospects of a sudden promotion, and the accompanying pay raise, the private priest became the spiritual adviser to the highest bidder.

The Danites' choice clearly contradicted the rule of God. Because the people did what was right in their own eyes, they easily exchanged the rule of God for the security they deemed best for themselves.

Many people still live by doing what is best in their own eyes. Often they truly do know what is right, but accomplishing it requires more than they are willing to invest. *They have exchanged status for security.*

Right is replaced with selfishness The Book of Judges spans three hundred years of Hebrew history. Throughout this time, the people repeated a pattern of behavior over and again—replacing superstition for true religion, security for God's rule, and selfishness for stability in God's love.

God sent seven judges to call the Hebrew nation back to himself. Each time a judge appeared, the people repented and returned. And just as soon as the judge was gone, the people again did what was right in their own eyes.

A different priest was living in the hill country and took a concubine. Priests were assigned to live inside the city walls and minister in the tabernacles. They also were not in the habit of taking concubines. But everyone, even the priests, did what was right in their own eyes.

When this man's concubine left him to find her pleasure with other men, he went to bring her home and found her in her father's house. After several days, they began their trip home, only to stop in an unfamiliar town for the night.

It was the custom of the day for travelers to wait in the town square for someone to come and take them in for the night. An old man took them to his home, but no sooner had they arrived when the men of the city knocked on the door, demanding that the old man send out the stranger so they might rape him.

Instead of handing over the stranger, the old man gave up his virgin daughter and the stranger's concubine to the men and told them, "Do whatever you want with these women, but leave the stranger alone."

In the morning, the priest went to leave and found his concubine dead, holding onto the threshold of the old man's door. He loaded her up on his donkey and traveled home. When he arrived, he took a large knife and cut her body into twelve parts and sent one part to each of the twelve tribes, along with the story of what had happened.

The theme of today's life is "whatever makes me happy is right." It matters little what truly is right, only what makes me happy. With this as the basis for morality, absolutes are limited and options for behavior are unlimited. The value of everything rides on each individual's personal experience. *We have swapped stability for selfishness.*

The Book of Judges documents the seemingly endless repetition of such behavior by the Hebrews. It also reveals to us the willful exchanges we make, trading genuine relationship with God for something we think is "right for me."

Ruth: Trust God in the midst of change

The central passage of Ruth also describes Ruth's loyalty and commitment to God, even in the midst of great change. She was married to a man for about ten years, and they lived in the same town as his parents and brother. About that time her father-in-law died, and shortly thereafter so did Ruth's husband and his brother. This left Ruth, her sister-in-law (Orpah), and her mother-in-law (Naomi) alone.

Naomi pleaded with the two young women to return to their homeland and take other husbands. Orpah did, but Ruth remained. And that brings us to the central verses of the Book of Ruth: "Do not urge me to leave you or turn back from following you; for where you go, I will go, and where you lodge, I will lodge. Your people shall be my people, and your God, my God. Where you die, I will die, and there I will be buried" (Ruth 1:16–17). In all of the Old Testament, Ruth stands out as a shining example of trust. Her life had been shaken to its core, and yet she would not go back on her commitment to Naomi and to God.

When the two women arrived in Bethlehem, Ruth went to work picking up the grain that harvesters leave behind. Thus she ended up in a field owned by a man named Boaz. She must have been attractive, because Boaz told his servants to pull grain out of their own bundles so Ruth could have whatever she needed.

Now Boaz happened to be a relative of Naomi, and it was the custom of those days that the closest relative would take a widowed woman as his wife and raise up children for the dead husband. Boaz followed the legal procedure of the day and bought the field that had belonged to Ruth's dead husband. With it he also bought the right for Ruth to become his wife. After the two married, Ruth conceived and gave birth to a son. This boy became the grandfather of the man who would later become the king of Israel—none other than David.

Think about it: Ruth's faithfulness looked as if it would

lead her into a life of poverty and beggary. Instead, it led her to a new land, a new husband, and a new heritage. Because of her trust in God, she became the great-grandmother of King David!

We are constantly surprised by life's twists and turns. But God is not shocked by anything that happens to us. While he was not responsible for the death of her husband, God did take that tragedy and turn it into good, simply because Ruth saw the event as an opportunity to trust him.

God is always calling us to trust him. The way to do

> **Think about it: Ruth's faithfulness looked as if it would lead her into a life of poverty and beggary. Instead, it led her to a new land, a new husband, and a new heritage.**

it may not be immediately clear, but the choice *is* clear. This decision of trust will have to be reaffirmed more than once; in fact, it will most likely require frequent reaffirmation, day by day. But it will let us see the things that only God can do.

Samuel, Kings, and Chronicles: Trust God to know how to live

The books of 1 and 2 Samuel, 1 and 2 Kings, and 1 and 2 Chronicles give us the history of many kings. But three of these kings, in particular, summarize the message of these six books. We will briefly examine the lives of Saul, David, and

Solomon as they demonstrate a great truth: We can trust God to know how to live.

Saul: Trust contaminated Saul was chosen to be the first king of Israel and was immediately welcomed by the people. He stood tall and strong, possessing great leadership qualities. For the first few years he ruled effectively, and the country prospered. But after a time, Saul became greedy for more power and wealth. For example, when God ordered him to go to battle against the Amalekites, he told Saul not to take any of the animals or wealth as booty. But after the battle, Saul *did* take the animals—and everything else that was good—and kept it all for himself. He even spared the Amalekite king's life.

This was just the beginning of Saul's compromising with God. The rest of his life was characterized by partially trusting God and then by completely forsaking his trust in God.

David: Trust consecrated This young shepherd boy learned how to trust God while watching over his sheep. When the bear would attack, he'd use his sling to kill it. When the lion would attack, he'd use his staff to defend the helpless sheep. Each time he fought off attacks, David realized his life was in danger. Nevertheless, he trusted God to deliver him.

David was chosen by the high priest Samuel as the next king of Israel. This is the same young man who stood before the giant Goliath and defeated him. He is the same young man who hid in the desert from Saul for years. He is the same man who once-and-for-all defeated the Philistines, Israel's archenemy. And he is the man who built Jerusalem into a great city. Sadly, this is also the same man who took another man's wife and had the husband killed.

However, when confronted by a prophet, David asked forgiveness for his sin and accepted the consequences without complaining. David's trust in God wasn't compromised, but it was consecrated. Throughout his days he trusted God.

Like all of us, sometimes David turned to himself rather than to God. But each time he turned his trust around and placed it squarely back on the Lord. In fact, God himself would say of David, "This is a man after my own heart."

Solomon: Trust compromised Solomon was David's son, who's greatest accomplishment was to build the Temple for Israel's worship. David had built prosperity and peace into Jerusalem, but Solomon built the Temple of the Lord. During the first years of his reign, Solomon sought the wisdom of God. Rulers from all over the world came to Solomon, bringing him great wealth for his wise advice. During this time Solomon wrote many of the Proverbs recorded in the Bible.

Later in his life Solomon's trust in God weakened. He took for himself many wives, along with four hundred concubines. He allowed

> "God reaches into our lives and asks the direct question: 'Will you trust me in the good times, the bad times, the easy times, and the hard times? Will you trust Me?'"

these women to bring into his home and his nation the worship of other gods. This not only infected true worship, it also caused his own trust in the true God to wane. During this time in his life, Solomon wrote the Book of Ecclesiastes, which is filled with examples of his wavering trust.

You and me: Trust chosen? All of us live with the influence of these three kings inside us. When it comes to trusting God, we're challenged to preserve fidelity. Like Saul we often want to take for ourselves the things God says to avoid. The compromise may seem insignificant at first, but unless it is rooted out, trust erodes.

We'll also face times of failure, like David, and choose whether to deny or repent. And there will be times when our trust will be conflicted, when we still want to maintain control when God invites us to let go.

The lesson of these three kings is for me and you. God reaches into our lives and asks the direct question: "Will you trust me in the good times, the bad times, the easy times, and the hard times? Will you trust me?" We can answer in any way we wish.

> " In addition, there was a little fine attached to breaking this rule: you'd have to die. "

Ezra, Nehemiah, and Esther: Trust God to know who you are

The books of Ezra, Nehemiah, and Esther convey the story of Israel in captivity. God's people have been carried away to Babylon as captives, their native land laid to waste.

Just as their ancestors got used to living in Egypt, these captives became content to remain in Babylon instead of returning to their real home. Only a handful could be persuaded into returning to rebuild the Temple and the city of Jerusalem.

These three books capture the spirit of the people during this time. They are morally distorted, socially disjointed, and economically destitute! But even in this low period, God began redeeming his people. He raised up Ezra and Nehemiah, who would lead groups back into their land to rebuild.

Amidst their desolation God still called out to the people, "Will you trust me?" He was looking for the ones who would trust him enough to return to the homeland. He wanted them to begin the arduous task of rebuilding the things they had lost seventy years earlier.

The Book of Esther tells of a beautiful Hebrew maid who became the queen in a foreign land. Strangely, even though Esther was queen, she wasn't allowed to drop in on the king any time she wished; instead, she could only come into his presence when summoned. In addition, there was a little fine attached to breaking this rule: you'd have to die.

Now for the condensed version of the action: One of the king's under-rulers, Haman, hated the Hebrews who lived among his people, so he sought to destroy them. Haman devised a secret plot to eliminate them. Meanwhile, Mordecai (who was Esther's uncle) discovered the plot and told Esther. After careful consideration, Esther decided to approach the king with Haman's wicked plan. Her life was at risk, of course, but here is what Esther said: "I will go to the king, even though it is against the law. And if I perish, I perish" (Esth. 4:16 NIV). This was truly a do-or-die mission.

It turned out the king was more interested in the plot than in maintaining the royal etiquette. He quickly dealt with Haman, putting an end to his plans of racial genocide. In an ironic twist, the king hung this evil plotter on the gallows Haman had built for Mordecai! The Jewish queen in captivity in a foreign land had responded to God's question, "Will you trust me?" Setting her own life aside, she saved her people from destruction.

These three books can be summarized in the following way. Ezra deals with the people's *disinterest*. They had become comfortable in their surroundings. Yes, they were captives, but they'd lost interest in trusting God to accomplish what he had promised in and through them. The Book of Nehemiah deals with the *disapproval* that comes whenever the God's people trust him to do everything he promises to do. And the Book of Esther addresses the way God's people deal with *deceit*, especially when it is aimed at destroying them and their work for the Lord.

The question God asked the people in captivity is the same he asks us: "Will you trust me?" We've all been in bondage to something or someone. We've all experienced what Israel felt: "It's just easier to stay where I am rather than go against the system. I'm not up for that kind of fight."

Should the difficulty lay in our own overt or latent disinterest, we must see it for what it is and willfully choose to deny ourselves the self-appointed right of comfort. We'll need to get about the task of trusting God. If the problem resides in our unwillingness to face the disapproval of others, perhaps we can look to Jesus and see that is exactly what he had to do. We can choose to follow in his footsteps. Or if the trouble is coming from the deceit of others, we must be wise and choose our actions carefully. Trusting God, we'll expose the deceit to those who can root it out. Let us allow nothing to keep us from answering God's call to trust him. Trust in God is our calling, our identity in Christ, our birthright. We were born to trust him.

Chapter Four

DO YOU HEAR ME?

We live in a society where most of the people under twenty-five have lost a basic command of the language. It seems that a new part of speech has been invented, and it's called, Assumptive Knowledge. You'll find an example in almost any sentence flowing from our young linguists' mouths: "So I went to the mall, *y'know what I'm sayin?*" This simple phrase seems to project immediate understanding into the listening party's brain.

After I finished speaking at a church one evening, a young man approached me with a smile on his face. I extended my hand to welcome his comments, and our conversation went something like this:

"Man, tonight was ... do you *feel* me?" he asked.

I looked at him, still shaking hands, and said through a staged smile, "No I really *don't* feel you. What do you think about tonight?"

"Aw man, it was ... *ya know what I'm sayin'?*"

I wondered how to keep that conversation going!

I do have a difficult time being too critical of this evolution of language, though. After all, this weekend, in hundreds of pulpits across the nation, many preachers will expound and proclaim, having spent little or no time in preparation. They will string words together, hoping people will get the gist of their half-prepared ideas.

In order to really "sell" the presentation, with the hope of evoking some response from the audience, they pepper their sentences with, "Give him some praise!" Or, "Give him some glory!" Which really means, "clap for what I just said."

This really is the Christianized version of, "Y'know what I'm sayin?" and it evokes the same response from those listening. They agree, because they don't want to appear stupid or act as if they aren't listening.

Throughout this section of the Bible, God continually asks: "Do you hear me?" There are times when humans *do* hear God's questioning, but most times they are the one's asking the same question of God: "Do *you* hear *me?*"

Job: Do you hear me ... in the messes of my life?

"Oh that I had one to hear me! Behold, here is my signature; Let the Almighty answer me! And the indictment which my adversary has written."

—Job 31:35

Within the first twelve verses of this book we discover something foundational to the understanding of good and evil in our world. The bad things that come upon Job come from the hand of Satan. God has absolutely nothing to do with Job's distress. This is the story behind the story of Job.

Satan's agenda competes with God's. Satan has to *de*-create everything God has created, and this includes us humans.

Everything was going great for Job, until one day his whole life disintegrated in crisis. In the midst of a satanic-induced chaos, Job came face to face with the deepest questions of life. Job's faith was tested to its depths, as was his personal ability to endure physical, emotional, and spiritual hardship. Job's three-stage experience tells us: We are not alone in the messes of life.

Ordered Life is good. Job had known nothing but success in his orderly life. In a very few years, he'd become extremely wealthy in lands, flocks, and family. It seemed that his future would just be more of the same. To top it all off, Job walked closely with God.

Disordered Something happens that creates distress in our otherwise orderly days. Job was going through his normal daily activities when one of his servants bursts in hollering that a neighboring people had come and attacked the servants watching over his livestock. They had killed the servants and stolen the animals. Before that servant finished, another servant entered, telling Job more attackers killed all the servants who cared for the camels—and stole all his camels. While that servant was still speaking, and before the first servant could leave, a third servant ran in to tell Job that all of his children had been killed in a surprise raid as they were partying.

Job's once orderly world had quickly fallen apart. His future was no longer bright.

Reordered A new reordering of our world takes place. For much of the book, Job and his friends present their cases as to why the bad things have happened to Job. The message behind the story does not resolve the blame (that was established in the first chapter of Job; Satan's the bad guy). But it does let us know that when disorder arrives, God knows it, hears us, and stands beside us. We may not hear him, not sense his presence, not recognize that he understands the situation. Nevertheless, God is there. He does not offer easy solutions, though. He doesn't offer any because there are no easy solutions to the disorder that hurtles toward us regularly.

> **We may not hear him, not sense his presence, not recognize that he understands the situation. Nevertheless, God is there.**

The solution God offers is *to come to the point that we clearly hear him* in the midst of the disorder. This is the way to reorder the disorder. We can find the calm in the chaos when we truly understand that God gets our problem and he gets us. The chaos presents no surprises to God; the pandemonium does not disturb his peace. The peace God carries with him is big enough to envelope everyone who will hear him in the midst of their own disorder.

"I have heard of You by the hearing of the ear; But now my eye sees You; therefore I retract, And I repent in dust and ashes." (Job 42:5–6). Job was now more ready to listen to God than to reason out why bad things happen. He stopped his questioning and ended his search for the easy answers; he simply took comfort in hearing from God.

A well-ordered life should not be our focus, nor should we zero in on the supposed "lessons" we can learn from the disorder of life. Our focus should be on hearing God. We humans ask our question of God every day: "God, do you hear me when I cry out in the messes of my life?" God's answer is the same question: "But don't you hear *me* in the disorder?"

Psalms: Do you hear me ... when I cry out?

The Book of Psalms is more than a collection of songs and prayers capturing particular moments in the lives of a few key leaders. These songs and poems had a permanent place in the life of Israel, providing them with vehicles to express a wide variety of emotions to God.

Let's look at Psalm 22 as an example. It is a *lament,* or a poem expressing extreme candor with God. A lament says: "God, we're desperate, and you are our only hope!" It's like throwing a "holy fit."

Throughout the Psalms, worshipers use laments to make their needs known to God. A lament arises out of the *pure* hearts of worshipers seeking to reaffirm the *faithfulness* existing between themselves and God. A lament is petitionary prayer condensed to its most basic form: "Help!" Here's an example: "Far from my deliverance are the words of my groaning. O my God, I cry by day, but You do not answer; And by night, but I have no rest" (Ps. 22:1–2). Such expressive encounters are void of pride or arrogance. They aren't shrouded with anger or injected with false piety.

No, these are words spoken out of a passionate commitment to maintaining the integrity of the most important relationship of life, the agreement between God and persons. The relationship of agreement is the most important thing to the speaker. He is coming to God in this way because he feels forsaken, left alone to his own resources. He knows he can't survive without the relationship, and he has come to set it right.

> **Sometimes God refuses to act until we learn to trust the indestructible nature of our relationship with him—and approach him with extreme candor.**

Sometimes God refuses to act until we learn to trust the indestructible nature of our relationship with him—and approach him with extreme candor. Our tendency is to remain passive. We try to accept without question everything that comes our way as something God himself has engineered. Or, at the very least, we assume that God had something for us to learn through it. Thus we miss out on some of the most powerful activities of God.

There are situations in life that will never be remedied until we become comfortable standing, without flinching, in the full upright position we have been given in Christ. And as we stand there, we will hold God accountable to his holiness. Do you pray that way? Such open-hearted candor with

God can only deepen our relationship. We are opening our true selves to him rather than "cleaning up first." And the deepened relationship yields added faith and resilience to withstand even greater troubles the next time around.

Proverbs: Do you hear me … as I figure life out?

Proverbs is God's character made practical and applicable to human life. Each verse contains a morsel of God's character sandwiched between two slices of instruction that provide two views of the *practical nature* of God's character. These two views are often held in tension with each other, and the character of God comes through in the midst of them.

I know that sounds a little complicated, so here's an example of what I mean. It's a verse that demonstrates the character of God sandwiched between two views of God: "The mind of man plans his way, But the LORD directs his steps" (Prov. 16:9).

God has given us a mind and expects us to use it to its fullest. He has created us with the capacity to think and to create plans to accomplish the purposes of life. We are to think through these processes and plan our way. But behind it all, through it all, and during it all, we are to realize that it is the Lord who directs our steps. *The character of God rests in the combination of these two statements.* As we apply it to our lives, it is the character of careful and thoughtful planning, of hard work, and quiet trust in God's direction.

The wisdom and truths found in Proverbs are much more than an anthology of behaviors God finds acceptable. They are outward expressions of the dynamic freedom available to everyone living in agreement with God. By themselves, the proverbs are too many and too difficult to regularly apply to life. But we can see them as the natural outflow of a life lived in agreement with God. They show us the character of God made alive in us and visible in practical attitudes and actions. Proverbs gives us three levels of practical, Christlike character:

Personal connection with God (chaps. 1–9) The proverbs bring us into direct contact with the character of God. Proverbs can be characterized as the tissue paper through which we trace our character against the Lord's character.

Practical choices for our everyday living (chaps. 10–24) The Book of Proverbs overflows with nearly every imaginable situation humans face. The character of God comes through in believable ways that we can transfer to our lives.

Promised consequences (chaps. 25–31) Living according to God's character produces consequences. We can depend on those consequences in specific life situations. The outcome of our attitudes, actions, and choices will be anticipated and expected.

Ecclesiastes: Do you hear me ... in my search for meaning?

The author of this Bible book, King Solomon, remains unmatched in discernment and wisdom. He truly heard God speak as he sought to discern life's ultimate purpose and meaning. In all of his searching, Solomon was crying out to be heard by God. And all the while he missed out on God's voice returning the question: "Do *you* hear *me* in the discernment of life?"

We all want our lives to count, to matter, and to carry some weight in the world. Each of us tries to satisfy this need through various self-centered searches—through relationships, career achievements, or the attainment of power. The problem is, God didn't design us to find life's purpose and meaning by using ourselves as the measuring rod of acceptability.

> "The problem is, God didn't design us to find life's purpose and meaning by using ourselves as the measuring rod of acceptability."

When self becomes the unconditional authority for meaning, we will, by default, come up short. We'll mistake almost anything as meaningful and purposeful.

Ecclesiastes is in the Bible because it is inspired ("God-breathed"). Yet it's also filled with statements of human wisdom that are off kilter. God obviously wanted those statements included, in order to show the limits of a purely human philosophy. Many of the statements are true. Others, of course, are not to be believed since they depict human folly and erroneous thinking. Let's look at two statements in the book where, as a mere human being, Solomon got it wrong.

Human-wisdom statement #1 "The fate of the sons of men and the fate of beasts is the same. As one dies so dies the other; indeed, they all have the same breath and there is no advantage for man over beast, for all is vanity" (Eccl. 3:19).

Here Solomon says there's no real difference between animals and humans. In reality, God has created us in his own image and given us a position a little lower than himself (see Ps. 8). Our search for meaning cannot be found apart from understanding our unique position in the created order. Nor can it be discovered outside of accountability for our choices, attitudes, and actions. We were created in God's image so we can experience the most intimate of relationships with our Creator. No other segment of creation has such an awesome opportunity.

Human-wisdom statement #2 "That which is has been already and that which will be has already been, for God seeks what has passed by" (Eccl. 3:15).

Solomon is saying that a person's relationship with God is totally irrelevant because God busies himself with things that are not present, not here and now. According to Solomon, we search in vain for a personal relationship with God. This futile view of our ability to relate with God accounts for the complete frustration pervading the book: "'Vanity of vanities,' says the Preacher, 'Vanity of vanities! All is vanity'" (Eccl. 1:2).

> **❝ The courtship is God saying to us, 'Do you hear my desire to spend the rest of eternity with you?' ❞**

The Book of Ecclesiastes presents the human search for meaning without factoring in the supernatural and divine. It is the human quest for identity apart from a Creator. It is man and woman *asking*, instead of *hearing*, "Do you hear me, in the discernment of life?"

Song of Songs: Do you hear me ... in my longing to connect?

Solomon wrote the Song of Songs as a personal worship poem that he sang to God. This uncensored Technicolor masterpiece plays almost in slow motion, causing even the seasoned Bible scholar to blush at the level of intimacy depicted between God and people. The Song of Songs is often described as a poem about human lovers. But this dims the beauty of its picture of the relationship between humans and God.

Throughout the book, God calls out: "Do you hear me, do you hear my desire to be intimate with you?" Likewise, the human side of this question is also easy to hear. "Do you hear my desire for intimacy with you, God?" This longing for intimacy comes through in four sections mirroring the natural phases of inter-human relationships.

The courtship (Song 1:1–3:5) This phase includes everything leading up to conversion. Intimacy is not immediate, but more often approached in steps. God makes his presence known to us, along with his purposes. He helps us realize that we've been created to cooperate with him in the fulfillment of his plan to redeem the cosmos. We, in turn, begin an involvement in his kingdom, making our own decisions regarding our future commitment to God. The courtship is God saying to us, "Do you hear my desire to spend the rest of eternity with you?"

United in marriage (Song 3:6–5:1) The marriage is conversion, the covenant, and the honeymoon. During this period everything is new and every experience unique. We anticipate the adventure and easily accommodate the requests of the other. In this period of the relationship, God is saying to us, "Do you hear my desire to be completely at one with you?"

The struggles of adjusting in marriage (Song 5:2–7:10) The relationship between God and mankind is hardly static. A struggle emerges out of our desire for self-direction and God's call to let go of our ego. As we encounter the pure and selfless motives of God, the struggle for intimacy escalates. God's plan for intimacy requires that we come into agreement with him. Through our repeated struggles with self-rule we feel the most discomfort in our growth toward intimacy with God. But as we learn to live within the challenge of the struggle, we grow close to him.

The journey (Song 7:11–8:14) The journey is the continued development of intimacy throughout all areas of our life, for the rest of life, as life unfolds. The wonder of intimacy with God is that we'll never fathom the depths of the relationship. It goes deeper and deeper.

The Song of Songs helps us see beneath the layers of veneer we've installed to insulate us from the vulnerability of intimacy with God. But as we lower our defenses, become honest and transparent with him, we experience the delights of his unconditional love. It is a level of intimacy with God—so authentic and connected—that it can only be likened to the sexual intimacy between a man and a woman.

Chapter Five

DO YOU SEE IT?

W hat would have happened if the Old Testament prophets had lost sight of their purpose? Suppose they started creating items to sell at their appearances for "ministry funding"? Imagine them trying to get their products in the hands of as many potential supporters as possible ...

- Isaiah, who had seen the Lord "high and lifted up" along with cherubim, would be selling small pewter replicas of the six-winged angels—suitable for either desk or dashboard.
- Jeremiah, who wore a wide leather belt and ate strange foods, would offer reproductions of his autographed, hand-tooled belts. (Comes with free 6-ounce bags of gourmet locusts.)
- Ezekiel would have his own line of chrome chariot wheels (they keep spinning, even after the chariot stops).
- Daniel would have developed a flame-resistant spray that could render virtually anything inflammable.

- Hosea might run a private detective company selling its services to anyone hoping to track down an unfaithful spouse.
- Jonah would have sold hand-carved scrimshaw (bone-carvings) depicting scenes of his life. He would have encouraged his supporters to collect all five scenes.

Thankfully, the biblical prophets never got off track like that! All sixteen stayed on target, constantly pointing people toward God. They each faithfully communicated the message that God was pursuing them for an intimate personal relationship: "Do you see it? God is passionate about you. He keeps seeking you out. Do you see it?"

The Old Testament prophetic books come in two varieties: the major and the minor prophets, simply depending upon the size of the book. These titles have nothing at all to do with the *importance* of the messages. There is, however, one contextual difference between the major and the minor prophets. The major prophets—Isaiah, Jeremiah, Ezekiel, and Daniel—mainly proclaim that God *will* deliver; they look for a change of heart in the people of Israel. The minor prophets proclaim the *method* of deliverance; they look for a change of hope.

In both cases, the prophets ask the crucial question: "Do you see it? God is seeking you out!" Each of the prophets asked this central question in his own way, according to the felt needs of their audiences. They presented the question in the form of a promise, something the people could believe. If God said it, then it was true, and it would surely come to pass.

The seventeen prophetic books of the Old Testament are

not as difficult to understand as once thought. At the outset, their message seems complex, but it is truly simple. Seventeen books, and seventeen promises that demonstrate seventeen different ways God remains true to himself and to his commitment to us. He created us and will do everything necessary to maintain relationship with us. Do you see it?

Isaiah: Promise of purity The people needed a new start, a new beginning. Isaiah told them that God would bring this newness to them by making all their sins as white as snow. But they must respond to this gracious Lord in genuine humility. Isaiah reminded the people of God's promise that he would raise up a pure people for himself. God continually sought them to be that pure people.

Jeremiah: Promise of parting The people had set out to make their own way apart from God's plans. They had trusted their own strength instead of God's, their own wisdom, their own direction, and their own resources. Jeremiah's message was simple and clear: When we try to match strength with God by placing our will over his, he will let us have our way. Then we end up wandering further and further into the darkness of selfishness.

"Because of your choices," said Jeremiah, "you have built a partition between yourselves and God." God's love allows us our choices, even when they're self-destructive. "Do you see it?" Jeremiah asked. "There has been a parting of ways between God and you!"

Lamentations: Promise of pain Jeremiah wrote this short book lamenting the destruction of Jerusalem. However, the

> **In the midst of our difficult situations and complex times, we must take responsibility for our wrong choices.**

lament applies to anyone suffering in the depths of neediness.

Five poems of lament address Israel in the hands of the Babylonians. No one swoops in and declares that everything will be all right. We find only a painful grieving over Jerusalem's devastation. The heart of the book is 5:20–21: "Why do You forget us forever? Why do You forsake us so long? Restore us to You, O LORD, that we may be restored; Renew our days as of old."

In the midst of our difficult situations and complex times, we must take responsibility for our wrong choices. Part of an authentic lament is repentance. There has to be a moment of clarity when we admit that we've violated God's will and shunned his love. This is radical honesty. It is painful, but its genuineness leads us to see God as he really is—in constant pursuit of us.

Ezekiel: Promise of presence The Book of Ezekiel ends with a word picture of God's temple, where God is at rest with his people. The prophet was making the point that we ourselves are the ultimate dwelling place of God. As God's presence grows in us, his influence expands around the world.

Daniel: Promise of participation Daniel was one of the finest young men Israel had to offer. That's why the Babylonians carried him off into leadership training in their own country. Even in this foreign land, Daniel honored God in everything he did.

Daniel was once discovered praying to God, when that was a crime in Babylon. When he was "punished by lion," God closed the mouths of those hungry cats and spared Daniel's life. The Book of Daniel shows how God participates in our lives in the most practical ways. (Also, it shows us the future of the world; check it out!)

•••

Beginning with Hosea, and continuing through Malachi, the Minor Prophets instill hope in the One who will personally inhabit human lives. No longer would daily sacrifices be needed; the Messiah's ultimate sacrifice would be forever placed in the hearts of those who accept him. The twelve statements below are *promises of the Hope who comes to live in us.*

Hosea: Promise of persistence God gave Hosea a strange assignment. He was to marry a woman who would be unfaithful to him! Then he must pursue her, redeeming her and bringing her back home. Why? Because his actions would symbolize how Israel—the unfaithful wife—had treated the One who loved and sought her. What was true for Israel is true for us today. Regardless of the ways we have treated God, he still seeks intimacy with us. Do you see it?

Joel: Promise of his purposes This book captures God at work in nearly every stratum of the cosmos. There is nothing he can't turn into good for the sake of everyone who loves him. When the problems of the world cause you stress and worry, read the Book of Joel. Over and over he asks, "Do you see it? God is at work, keeping the promise

> **God does not grade on the curve! Nor does he alter his standard according to the difficulty of the situation at hand.**

that his purposes will never fail."

Amos: Promise of perfection God calls Amos to place a plumb line against the nation of Israel. A plumb line measures how close to "straight and narrow" an individual and a nation has walked. The message here is that God does not grade on the curve! Nor does he alter his standard according to the difficulty of the situation at hand. Our tendency is to say that we have done our best, and that should be enough.

But our best is never enough. God will not be content until our lives line up exactly with the plumb line of his perfection. "Do you see it?" God loves us so much that he gives us the Perfect Sacrifice who meets the standard on our behalf. Then, in humble gratitude, we spend the rest of our lives pursuing personal, practical holiness.

Obadiah: Promise to prevail Throughout its history, Israel had been on and off with God, hot and cold. But Obadiah tells us we can overcome that pattern. When we feel weak, incapable of maintaining fidelity with God, this prophet's message strengthens our faith to keep holding on. We want God to rule and reign in every part of our lives, but we are our own worst enemy. Yet God will enable us to prevail over the evil and fleshly influences in our lives. All we have to do is look for his provision. It's there, but do we see it?

Jonah: Promise of preservation Don't just focus on the big fish! The central story of Jonah is that "the word of the Lord came to Jonah *a second time.*" Yes, our Lord is the God of second chances, promising preservation. But just like Jonah, we need to look for this part of God's character. Too often we fail to see it. Therefore, Jonah's question is for us today: "Do you see it? Do you see the God of preservations; the God of repeat chances?"

Micah: Promise of pardon The central verse of the Book of Micah is 6:8, "What does the Lord require of you? To act justly and to love mercy and to walk humbly with your God" (NIV). The intent of this verse is not to establish minimal behavior standards. Rather, it is to remind us all that no one is capable of meeting even this most basic standard. Micah tells us that God will pardon all who ask forgiveness for their failures. Every one of us has fallen short of God's commands, and every one of us needs pardoning. God's promise waits for everyone who will see it and come to receive it.

Nahum: Promise of patience God is motivated more by the fulfillment of his purposes than he is by love. That is, love directs everything he does toward fulfilling his purposes. His love leads God to be patient with us as we grow in our abilities to understand and live in his purposes. The promise of patience is real, but patience doesn't require an

> **The promise of patience is real, but patience doesn't require an endless tolerance of rebellion.**

endless tolerance of rebellion. There is a point at which even God's patience will end. Unless his people humble themselves and turn from their selfish and wicked ways, God's judgment will fall.

Habakkuk: Promise of provision This prophet wondered, as we do: *How can God, who is just, allow injustice to continue? How can he allow the poor and innocent to suffer? And why does he let the oppressors enjoy their riches?*

The answer is that God will provide everything we need—even an ultimate justice.

This is not the easy answer it seems. It does not encourage the deaf ear or a blind eye to people's sufferings. Yet we need not be overwhelmed by the problems and injustices of the world; God remains in control. The prophet calls us always to see life from this point of view. Habakkuk cries out to God for us all: "God, do you see what we see?"

Zephaniah: Promise of protection Many people say they can't accept a God who responds with anything other than tender, compassionate love. They can't accept the type of divine wrath Zephaniah proclaims. But the compassionate love of God also has a stern, prohibitive side that protects us from self-destruction.

In the same way a loving parent says "No" to a child flirting with danger, so God lets us see his disapproval of some of our requests. Sometimes only a forceful, dramatic "NO!" will get our attention. The goal is protection. This is the nature of God's wrath. Do you see it? He loves us so much that he will protect us from the things that might harm our relationship with him.

Haggai: Promise of prosperity The Book of Haggai identifies a link God placed between the physical and the spiritual. In the Old Testament, physical prosperity mirrors spiritual prosperity. Therefore, the prophet told people that if they felt they could never "get ahead" financially, they ought to look into their spiritual condition. Specifically, they ought to realize it was wrong to live in their comfortable houses when the house of God remained unfinished.

They had forgotten God and the rebuilding of his temple. They had become obsessed with building their own homes and acquiring acceptable societal trappings. They had forgotten their central identity as God's people; therefore, they had forgotten that God is the source of true prosperity. That's why they felt poor, as if their money was always running out:

"You have planted much, but have harvested little.
You eat, but never have enough. You drink, but never
have your fill. You put on clothes, but are not warm. You
earn wages, only to put them in a purse with holes in it."
—Haggai 1:6 (NIV)

Haggai said: "Put God at the center of your lives, and watch your prosperity increase." God speaks to all believers through this book. He sees us and knows that we will only feel satisfaction in life when our spirits rest in him.

Zechariah: Promise of pre-eminence At first reading, this prophet seems to be the master of bad-news delivery. Zechariah heralds world judgment, much as it's depicted in Revelation. But the message behind the message is: "Regardless of how bad things get, God will reign."

This book is our reminder that, when things seem their darkest, the world appears to be falling apart, and God is about to take a fall ... *all is not as it may appear.* The One who draws us to his side will never go down in defeat. Zechariah provides us with the promise of God's pre-eminence. He always rules, always stays in command.

Malachi: Promise of proximity In four short chapters, this prophet reveals the condition of all humankind—

"You have forgotten Me."

"You have robbed Me."

"You have said harsh things about Me."

And with each of these accusations, God draws closer and closer to the part of his creation he fashioned in his own image. The Book of Malachi reveals to us the God who makes certain that every individual has the opportunity to the greatness of divine love. God breaks into our lives and communicates his love to each of us, *in the way that we can understand and accept.* The promise of this prophet is the promise of God's proximity with us, in us, and through us. This book is the fitting conclusion to the Old Testament, as it perfectly lays the groundwork for the coming of the Christ.

Everything God set into motion throughout the Old Testament, he continued to work out through the lives of people between the conclusion of Malachi and the beginning of Matthew. Whether or not people could see his work, God was constantly bringing about his will on the face of the earth and in the lives of mankind.

Interlude: What's happening when God is silent?

Waiting. Why does it take so long?

Here's what I mean: When I go to the grocery store, I never get more than a few items. (That's because I'm never in one place long enough for a quart of milk to go bad, much less a carton of yogurt.) But without fail, in almost any city I'm in, I can take my two or three items to the "Ten Items or Less" checkout lane and wait behind at least two of the severely mathematically challenged. They are clearly in the ten-or-less line, but they have half a cart full.

One time a guy turned to me and justified his actions this way: "See, everything falls into only nine different ... *categories.*" (His "fruit" section, for instance, included apple pie, lime sherbet, and a big bag of cherry LifeSavers. And I never

> ❝ Most of us believe that nothing of real value comes from waiting. Even though this isn't true, we still hate to wait. ❞

realized the cream filling in Twinkies really was a dairy product.) I could feel my eyes rolling back into my head. All I could think to say was, "Would you please hurry up? I have at least three other places where I should be waiting right now!"

Most of us believe that nothing of real value comes from waiting. Even though this isn't true, we still hate to wait, because it seems little of significance happens while we stand tapping our toes. So imagine how God's people must have felt during the four hundred years between the Old Testament days and the New Testament days.

During this period, God's voice was silent—no new prophetic pronouncements. Yet God was active. He was putting every piece of his plan in place so that, at just the right time, he could install his answer for the sins of mankind: his own Son, Jesus.

We can observe God's activities during these four hundred years of silence in four different areas of society. Each of these areas had to be prepared to receive God's solution for the sin of mankind.

Politically During these four hundred years, the Greeks invaded Israel, along with most of the civilized world. The Greeks brought with them their language, their philosophy, and their spirit of love for truth and reason. Many of these Greek qualities began to make their way into the Hebrew culture.

During the later years of this interlude, the Romans came and conquered the Greeks, taking possession of their lands (including Israel). Over the next several decades, they spread their infrastructure throughout the land. They brought with them a strong central government and built permanent roads, aqueducts to supply water, and established inter-city trade via land and sea. The Romans made it possible to travel to any part of the known world. While they brought all these advancements, they also allowed the Jewish religion to flourish and expand. Synagogues sprouted in nearly every city throughout the Roman Empire.

In a growing cosmopolitan world, the Hebrews continued

to worship one God rather than accept the popular polytheistic idolatry. The nation of Israel worshiped the Lord, who was in relationship with them. During this period of time, three religious groups emerged within the religious society: the Sadducees, the Pharisees, and the Scribes. Each of these represented separate Jewish sects, and each had their own ideas about the identity and mission of the Messiah.

Philosophically During this time, people generally believed the earth filled the center of the universe. Furthermore, every event on earth resulted from the struggle between good and evil, which were constantly in conflict. There was a profound sense of human unworthiness and an extreme dissatisfaction with the present. People longed for help beyond the purely human realm.

Prophetically The prophetic time table of Daniel 2:36–40 predicted that an iron kingdom would come and crush all others. The Romans had defeated all other nations and unified the world under their rule. Thus the Roman empire made it possible for the Kingdom of Christ to come and to be supercharged as it spread throughout the world. Galatians 4:4 says that "in the fullness of time" God did things beyond human control to create a worldwide environment suitable for implanting His Son into human history. The scheme of world events had been prepared to receive God's ultimate expression of love.

Personally We've all experienced times of wondering whether God has forgotten us. We feel alone, untouched, and unnecessary. The inter-testament period spanned four hundred years in which God's voice was not heard. Yet his hand was working to shape the perfect circumstances for his living Word to enter the world. The same is true in our lives. Even when we feel abandoned, we are not alone. God is at work, engineering circumstances for the delivery of his Word right into the center of our lives.

Chapter Six

WHERE IS THE LOVE?

One of Jesus' most notable sermons was, of course, his Sermon on the Mount. But imagine if he were here, in today's culture, to deliver it. He's speaking at an outdoor amphitheater ...

When he stands to speak someone from the back pitches a blue, white, red, and green beachball into the air, sending it spinning in all directions as the crowd keeps it airborne. Jesus' tag-along brother, John, shows up wearing a rainbow afro wig and a bright yellow T-shirt with the slogan "Me 3:16." John turns to the person next to him and says, "Everybody thinks I'm crazy for wearing it. But I'm telling you, one day it's going to catch on."

Just as Jesus finishes with the "Blessed are those who" section of the sermon, a man answers his cell phone and starts talking too loudly. "Yeah, man. The dude is talking about ways to be happy. He's an okay speaker, just not very deep."

Just as Jesus begins expounding on salt and light, a man strolls to the front holding up a poster board with the name of a child whose parents need to come and pick him up. Jesus pauses, and waits for the announcement: "Will the parents please pick up their son? He just threw up, and we're out of the orange pencil-shaving floor absorbent. You can pick him up behind the guy who's speaking." The crowd is only slightly distracted, and Jesus picks up where he left off ... .

Thankfully, Jesus didn't have to break into human history amidst today's entertainment crowds! When he delivered the Sermon on the Mount, times were much simpler. For the most part, people were also more polite.

Jesus broke into history and demonstrated to all humankind that he is the fulfillment of all the prophetic predictions. He is our redeemer and liberator, the one who will always be with us. When the world was asking God, "Where is the love?" he heard and answered with Jesus. When God asks the world, "Do you know where the love is?" he expects the world to answer with the same name.

The four books known as Gospels reveal different aspects of Jesus the Christ. When put together, they provide us with a composite portrait that is both accessible and personal.

Matthew: Jesus is the king of the Jews

Matthew spoke to his own Jewish people, presenting them with their king. He writes to highlight Jesus' kingly position, authority, and power. But many of the religious people in his audience were actually spiritual elitists, insiders who believed they'd already attained everything they needed. They certainly didn't see themselves in need of Jesus; they already had God's Law in their Bible (the first five books of the Old Testament).

Because of this mindset, Matthew repeatedly shows Jesus confronting the ultra-religious culture in Judaism. Jesus takes on the religious substructure that felt threatened by his very presence. He reveals the futility of legalism's efforts to bring people closer to God through sheer effort and good works. He confronts the exclusive nature that a pharisaic Judaism had adopted, shattering it with his unqualified invitation to all peoples, regardless of race or creed.

Matthew presents Jesus as a subversive figure to the super-religious mind. Everything these folks had come to know about religion began to seem out of place positioned beside the person and teaching of Jesus. They were looking for a messiah to come and fulfill their preconceptions—not to challenge them.

The announcement of the King Matthew begins with a detailed list of Jesus' ancestors, going all the way back to King David. The Hebrew people knew the Old Testament prophecy that the Messiah would come from David's bloodline. So Matthew took great care to demonstrate for everyone that Jesus was the Son of David. Matthew was really answering the question "Where is the love?" by showing that dwelt in the person of Jesus Christ.

The authority of the King In Matthew, Jesus demonstrates his authority over the physical realm. One evening he and his disciples set out across the Sea of Galilee in a small boat. Later that night, while the disciples were rowing, a strong storm arose. But Jesus was sleeping in the rear of the boat. The disciples tried to manage the boat themselves, but quickly discovered they were no match for the storm. They woke Jesus, who stood and spoke to the storm: "Peace, be still!" The winds and sea obeyed him.

Matthew shows Jesus exercising authority over physical diseases as well, including demon possession. Everything Jesus did flowed from his heavenly authority and his love for mankind.

The audacity of the King Jesus confronts Jewish religious traditions head on. These traditions had often become heartless and loveless, enshrining regulations impossible to keep. Jesus taught that these laws failed, not because they were too strict; rather, they weren't strict enough! For example, their religious traditions said "Don't murder." But Jesus taught that anyone enraged against his brother had already committed murder in his heart. The audacity! But here's the point: If perfection really is the standard, then our only hope is to cling to a perfect Savior who takes our place before the divine Judge.

Jesus knew that the religious leaders were motivated by a fear of losing their positions, not by love. He had the audacity to stand up to them in public and openly teach the true doctrine of love rather than legalism. Only the King of love could do this as Jesus did.

Mark: Jesus is the action-oriented servant

In Mark we see Jesus as a servant moving quickly from place to place. Mark writes to the Romans who occupied the Holy Land at this time. The Roman mind was pragmatic and viewed this Jesus as a novelty. Yet many Romans listened to his teachings because they were so different from current philosophy. The Romans at least had an open mind to Christ, so Mark wrote his Gospel to those who would say, "I'll try it."

Like the Jews—or any of us—Romans hungered for an unconditional acceptance. In their own ways, they too asked the question, "Where is the love?"

Although addressing a pragmatic audience, Mark presents his story in an unpragmatic way. He depicts Jesus in a fluid motion, moving almost spontaneously from location to location, healing diseases, delivering from evil spirits, and constantly teaching. Jesus does all of this without seeking personal reputation. In fact, he often commands the healed ones not to tell anyone what happened. Romans who desired expanded reputations would find this a strange approach.

> **We hide our fears and hurts behind layers of makeup and colored contact lenses. We dress up the outside, giving the illusion that our inner life is also well kept.**

Mark presents the loving actions of God through the selfless activities of Christ, culminating in his sacrificial death. On the cross, "no one takes his life away from him, but he willingly lays it down." In Mark, wherever Jesus went he met the true needs of mankind.

Like the Roman citizens, we, too, live in a society where our true needs lie hidden behind a disguise of affluence. Many of us have bankrupt souls, though we drive late-model cars and dress in the latest fashions. We hide our fears and hurts behind layers of makeup and colored contact lenses.

We dress up the outside, giving the illusion that our inner life is also well kept. In reality, we desperately seek someone to love us from the inside out. Christ's presence still moves many to open their hearts. They dare to take him at his word and say along with the Romans, "I'll try it."

Luke: Jesus is the Son, a compassionate healer

Luke presents Jesus as the Son of Man. Luke wrote his account to the Greeks, who were idealists. Their whole philosophy rested upon the vision of an ideal citizen who could live in an ideal place: the city. There one would find the perfection of human existence. These people knew of Christ but said, "I don't need it."

To the Greeks, love could be found only inside their idealism, even though it was filled with polytheism and the human attempt to please unappeasable gods. Luke's attempt was not to prove that Jesus was God; the gods were nothing new for the Greeks. Thus Luke stressed that *God became man.*

The Greeks and their idealism were a tough sell for the message of Jesus as the Son of Man. Luke tells them that Jesus is capable of understanding the needs of mankind because he himself was a man. Luke debunks the myth of religion and mankind's need to somehow reach acceptability with God through his own efforts. He clearly demonstrates how God came to earth to provide a way to heaven that people can't produce on their own.

Christ was born like every other man, and he grew into young adulthood like other men. In Luke Jesus' lineage goes all the way back to Adam, further linking him to the human race. Jesus was tempted like other humans, yet each time he emerged without sinning. He lived with the common man and ministered to his common needs.

Luke was a physician, so he was especially interested in Jesus' healing power. He shows Jesus healing on the Sabbath, bringing humanity to an inhumane religion. Jesus healed a slave, a blind man, a leper. He even raised a peasant mother's son from the dead.

He traveled throughout the land, bringing his healing touch of word and miracles to people everywhere he stopped. When John the Baptist sent two of his disciples to question this rabbi, Jesus said that they should return and tell John what they saw, "Go and report to John what you have seen and heard: the BLIND RECEIVE SIGHT, the lame walk, the lepers are cleansed, and the deaf hear, the dead are raised up, the POOR HAVE THE GOSPEL PREACHED TO THEM" (Luke 7:22).

As the Son of Man, Jesus identifies with human suffering and brings liberation to mankind. Luke's account of Jesus' life shows him bringing restoration to everything humans had lost because of their sin. This account is so clear that the idealists among us can clearly see our need for Christ.

John: Jesus is the one to believe

John is the Gospel of belief. Here Jesus comes through as the Son of God who calls us to believe in him. John was written to everyone—that is, anyone who could say, "I might be open to it."

John uses a unique approach to communicate the truth of Jesus to willing listeners. He writes of seven miracles that reveal the love of God through the activities of Christ. Next he recalls seven statements Jesus makes that reveal that he is love. And finally he reports seven unique interpersonal encounters Jesus had with people where the individuals either accepted or rejected his love.

The seven miracles Here are the miracles with a comment about what they taught:

• *Water changed to wine:* Newness of life that would come through him.

• *A nobleman's son—healed from a distance:* The faith required to receive Jesus and his love.

• *The healed paralytic:* How Jesus' strength replaces our weakness.

• *The multitude fed—from a kid's lunchbox:* The spiritual sustenance Jesus provides all who receive him and his love.

• *Walking on water:* How Jesus overcomes evil in the life of everyone who accepts him.

• *Sight restored to a blind man:* How Christ overcomes darkness and brings light to all who will believe.

• *Raising Lazarus from the dead:* Jesus' victory over death—and the eternal life he gives to everyone who receives him.

The seven "I am" statements First, realize: *Jesus claimed to be God.* The most important "I am" statement is ... "I AM." It's a name God applied to himself (see Exod. 3:14). In applying this statement to himself in John, Jesus also claimed to exist *before* Abraham (see John 8:58), something only possible for an eternal being. Now I'll just list the seven other statements, with their chapters ...

- *I am the Bread of life*: chapter 6.
- *I am the Light of the World:* chapter 8.
- *I am the Door:* chapter 10.
- *I am the Good Shepherd: chapter* 10.
- *I am the Resurrection and life:* chapter 11.
- *I am the Way, the Truth and the Life:* chapter 14.
- *I am the True Vine:* chapter 15.

The seven loving encounters Jesus meets lots of people in the Gospel of John. These encounters are especially poignant and instructive for us today.

- *Nicodemus.* In the middle of the night Jesus met Nicodemus, a religious leader with a personal interest in discovering just who Jesus was. He had heard Jesus speak and had requested a meeting to discuss his teachings more fully. Jesus could have required Nicodemus to meet with him during the daylight hours and in a public place where everyone could have seen them. Instead, Jesus agreed to meet with Nicodemus in private. Why? To allow him the necessary privacy to honestly discuss his need. In this encounter, Nicodemus found the acceptance and unconditional love that his religion could never offer.

- *The Samaritan woman.* Jesus told his disciples to go ahead of him into town, and he would wait by the town well for their return. While he waited, a woman came to draw water. She came in the heat of the day when everyone else would stay inside, so Jesus knew she was the subject of much gossip. They spoke candidly about her former marriages as well as her current "live-in" relationship. Jesus never judged

> **All they knew was that he was calling them to follow him, even to death. A great many of his followers then left him.**

her for her lifestyle, nor did he require her to treat him with any forced respect. Instead, he spoke kindly to her and helped her see that the way she was living harmed her and others. In this encounter, she found the love she had spent her entire life looking for.

• *The dividing of the disciples.* Jesus never pretended that following him would be easy. He had no home, and he had no regular place to sleep. Those who followed him would leave everything behind. The result of their sacrifice? They'd witness Jesus' healings, his teachings, and his compassion for people.

But one day Jesus' words caused a division among the disciples. He had been talking about his death in veiled terms that many didn't understand. All they knew was that he was calling them to follow him, even to death. A great many of his followers then left him.

Jesus turned to the twelve that he himself had chosen, and he asked them whether they, too, would leave. They chose to stay, because he alone had the words of life. This encounter reveals that Jesus' love is so pure and secure that he willingly allows anyone to choose whether or not they will follow him. It also reveals the reason anyone continues following him: They deeply believe that he alone has the words of life and love.

• *The woman taken in the act of sin.* One day while Jesus and his disciples were walking through town, the religious leaders approached and threw a woman at his feet. They had just caught her in the act of adultery. They stood there, stones in hand, ready to pass judgment and execute her. First they asked Jesus, "What do *you* say we should do with this woman?" Jesus stooped to the ground and wrote in the dirt. He stood back up and looked at the religious leaders, saying to them, "Whoever is without sin, go ahead and throw the first stone." The words stopped them cold.

• *The washing of the disciples' feet.* This was during the final supper Jesus would eat with his twelve closest friends before he went to the cross. They gathered in an upper room, and as they took their places, the disciples began to argue among themselves about just who would wash their feet before the meal. (Servants would normally do this—but no servants were there!)

No one was willing to humble himself to do the task of a menial slave, so Jesus did it. He took off his outer garment and wrapped the towel around his waist. Taking the bowl of water, he went to each of his disciples and washed his feet.

This encounter demonstrated his intense commitment and love. He willingly became their servants that they might learn to serve one another. Ultimately, the servant of us all willingly took on the sin of us all as the perfect, sinless sacrifice on the cross.

• *Mary Magdalene.* Three days after Jesus' crucifixion, Mary Magdalene, along with Peter and John, came to the tomb to anoint his body with spices. When they arrived at the garden tomb, the stone covering the entrance had been rolled away—and the tomb was empty.

Mary remained outside the tomb, amazed that someone would have come and taken Jesus' body. Then someone spoke to her from behind: "Woman, why are you crying?"

She thought it was the gardener and turned to ask him: "If you have moved the body, please tell me where I can find it." Mary was so overcome with grief that she didn't recognize the man. Then he spoke her name, and she immediately realized it was Jesus.

This encounter is the returning of honor to Mary. She is likely the one caught in the act of adultery, the one who washed Jesus' feet with her tears, and now she is the one receiving the firsthand report of the resurrection from Jesus himself.

• *Thomas.* The disciples were hiding after Jesus' death. They had been holed up for several days when the report came from the tomb: Jesus had risen. Thomas, though, said he just couldn't believe until he touched Jesus for himself.

Would we have acted like doubting Thomas? If we had walked with Jesus as he did, surely we wouldn't have doubted when we heard of his resurrection, right? But Thomas *did* question the validity of the resurrection reports; that is, until one day not long after, when Jesus walked through a wall to stand in front of Thomas. Jesus invited him to reach out and touch him, to examine his scars until he was satisfied. Immediately Thomas fell to his knees and confessed that Jesus had indeed risen from the dead.

This encounter reveals the patient and understanding

love that Jesus gives to us. He allows us the freedom to be completely honest, to bring our doubts and questions before him, to show him who we really are.

The cross and resurrection present an unshakeable apex to this chapter on the Gospels. The approach of each Gospel differs slightly, the perspective varies, and the accounts are uniquely directed to various audiences. Yet the stories are the same, each adding details that make a full picture of the One who died in our place. The Gospels demonstrate the thoroughness of God's quest: He makes certain that all persons everywhere know just how much he loves them.

> " He allows us the freedom to be completely honest, to bring our doubts and questions before him, to show him who we really are. "

Chapter Seven

WHAT AM I GOING TO DO WITH YOU?

We all know that men hate stopping their cars to ask for directions. In fact, surveys reveal that a man will spend one-third of his life listening to a woman say, "Well then, pull over and *I'll* ask!"

Then there's the issue of reading a map. Have you noticed that men won't read maps either? That's because they don't know how to re-fold them. It's a game; there are thirty-two ways to fold a map ... and only one of them is correct.

The books of the Bible from Acts through James are known as the Epistles. Some people think the Epistles were the wives of the apostles, but that's not true. Actually, they were letters written to the early churches because people in those churches needed to know how to live. I prefer to think of the Epistles as maps showing us how to live a faith that is practical and believable, rather than a faith that is contrived and unnatural.

If, when we think about God, we wonder, "What am I going to do with you?" we can be sure he's thinking the same about us! The Epistles are the roadmaps that help us know *what to do with God*—based upon all that God has already done with us.

The historical presentation

The Book of Acts reveals the history of the church's beginning. Just a couple of weeks after Jesus ascended from the earth and returned to heaven, the disciples were doing exactly what Jesus told them to do. They are waiting in Jerusalem until what he had promised came to them: the Holy Spirit.

In an upper room they had spent days in prayer and waiting on God. Suddenly the Spirit showed up and empowered each of them with supernatural gifts for ministry. That day Peter stood and preached to the crowd that had gathered. When he had finished, the Bible says the hearers were cut to the heart by the message. One question pressed upon them: "What am *I* going to do with Jesus?" The disciples ministered to those seekers, and three thousand accepted Christ. The New Testament church was born.

The church was an infant organism with inexperienced leadership. The disciples didn't know what to expect when Jesus told them to wait, but they were handed a living, breathing organism called the church, and he expected them to lead it. They looked at this new creation and wondered, "What am I going to do with you?"

Over the next few weeks, the church grew, and so did its reputation among the religious leaders of Jerusalem. Every day the church grew in size and influence. This inevitably led to persecution.

The religious leaders of Jerusalem didn't know what to do

with this new group claiming Jesus as their Messiah. They couldn't support this group and maintain their own positions of leadership, so they opposed it, even persecuted it. In the face of this opposition and persecution, the church grew even stronger!

Saul emerged on the scene as a zealot bent on preserving the traditional Hebrew religion. He traveled throughout the land, carrying with him the authority of the Chief Priest to seek out and persecute anyone claiming to be a believer in this Jesus.

Nor did the rest of society know how to handle this new religious group. The behavior of these believers was so counter-cultural that working with them proved to be a challenge. The new believers themselves faced new and unexpected challenges trying to work in a society that little appreciated Christ's values.

Acts was written by Luke, who brings a necessary realism to his writings; he wanted to convey all the important details of a growing organism. In these few chapters we get all the salient events that prove to be a perfect backdrop for the rest of the New Testament writings. Without the Book of Acts, the Epistles would be very difficult to understand, and the history of the early church would be a vague patchwork.

Acts serves as a historical transition from the Gospels to the Epistles, from Judaism to Christianity. It reveals the divine transition from law to grace. It transitions the identity of the people of God from Jews alone to include both the Jews and the Gentiles. And it identifies God's transition from a *heavenly* kingdom to a focus on building his kingdom through the *earthly* church.

The New Testament church understood the promises of God as uniquely theirs. The only Bible they had was the Old Testament, because the New Testament had not yet been written. These new believers saw every one of the prophecies as fulfilled in Christ. They saw themselves as the true Israel and, as such, recipients of the promises made in the Old Testament.

Over the months and years, the church continued to expand in influence and numbers. New believers were continually added, regardless of the persecution. Acts shows this growth, and the Epistles follow this growth to detail some of the growing pains the church encountered. They wondered what to do with each other, what to do with their growing notoriety, and what to do with the influence they began to wield on society.

> **Because of God's gracious work to make us his children, go ahead and live like children of the King! Become in practice who you are in position.**

The value of the Epistles to the first-century church, and to the church today, cannot be estimated. In these letters, many of the universal problems the church has already faced—and will yet face—are addressed with wisdom and insight. These insights continue to guide church members and leadership alike. Paul wrote nine letters to churches and four to individuals. These books of the Bible offer a large amount of doctrine. But it is doctrine dressed in practical clothing not theoretical smoke and mirrors. In fact, most of the Epistles begin with doctrine—telling us what God has done for us. Then they say: because of God's gracious work to make us his children, go ahead and live like children of the King! Become in practice who you are in position. We can organize the Epistles into three groupings to help us grasp their theme flow:

- Romans through Galatians: deal with the principles of following Christ.
- Ephesians through Philemon: deal with our position in Christ.
- Hebrews through Jude: deal with the practical connection of Christ's life to the circumstances of our own lives.

The principles of following Christ

Romans: Believe what God has said about you This book has been called the Genesis of the New Testament because it contains all the fundamental doctrine built upon in the rest of the Epistles. Paul is teaching all believers a new vocabulary of faith, a new way to think about and to process the Christian life. It is the fundamental book of the New Testament, showing what God is doing with us. Whenever we need to be reminded of what we are supposed to do with God, Romans is the place to go.

This Epistle reveals how God applies Christ's work on the

cross to us—in order to declare us righteous, acceptable, justified in his sight. It uncovers how Jesus' resurrection from the dead creates in us a new life as God changes us from the inside out. And it shines light on the way Christ's indwelling Spirit, ultimately transforms us into new creatures, citizens of heaven. Romans explains how the news about Jesus Christ was always intended to include everyone: Jews, Gentiles, and the entire world. Paul makes it clear that the way Abraham connected with God is the same way we connect with God, by the simple act of trust. The Book of Romans contains the kernel of every doctrine explaining what God is doing with us and what we are to do with him.

First Corinthians: Let go of what's hurting you This letter confronted certain problems in the young church of Corinth. Even though the congregation had only existed a few short years, it had developed problems that churches still face to this very day. Some members wanted to stir up strife in the fellowship. Some were openly immoral with sex, and others were suing each other in court! People were even being gluttons and getting drunk at the Lord's Supper. All these things were damaging the influence the church in society.

In this letter you can almost hear Paul's parental nature calling out, "What am I going to do with you guys? You are not acting as believers should act!"

In the first eleven chapters, Paul deals with the things that can and do hurt the church. In fact, he tells us all what will kill the church. In the final chapters, he shows how to remedy these problems and how to prevent them from returning. Every bit of the confrontation and correction Paul offers stands upon the underpinning of Christ's resurrection. Because Christ conquered death and the grave, he has given us his life and strength to live a new life in the Spirit. We have the life of Christ living in us; if we will listen to his life in us, we will know what to do.

Second Corinthians: Stay in agreement with the God who loves you Later in the life of this church in Corinth, false prophets arrived and worked hard to undermine all that Paul had worked to establish. They cast suspicion on Paul's character, his calling, and his credentials as an apostle. This caused the church to regress into former behaviors that Paul had addressed in his first letter.

In the midst of these huge problems, Paul refused to defend himself against the attacks. Instead, he went right to the heart of the matter: "[God] has made us competent as ministers of a new covenant—not of the letter but of the Spirit; for the letter kills, but the Spirit gives life" (2 Cor. 3:6 NIV).

This entire letter demonstrates that the very accusations leveled at Paul were also directed at all believers. The *character* of all believers is the life of Christ who lives in them. The *call* of all believers is to maintain their agreement with the dynamic plans of God, regardless of the circumstances of life they find themselves in. And the only *credential* any believer has is the new life Jesus places in him. Old things are passing away; all things are becoming new. It is the Spirit of God living in us who gives us life, who gives us the insight of what to do amidst all this world throws at us.

> 66 The question is: What do we do with the life of Christ and the dangerous freedom that comes with it? 99

Galatians: Live free in the life Christ gives you

The churches in Galatia had fallen into the trap of legalism. Legalism is the idea that keeping all the rules will save us. It has nothing to do with the freedom Christ gives all believers. We have the liberty to experience the fullness of his life within a world that is being redeemed by his power and grace. Legalism demands conformity to specific behaviors that have been canonized as holy. Such a lifestyle supposedly keeps one from being contaminated by a lost and fallen world. It also, however, keeps one from living by the Spirit or by the law of love.

The question is: What do we do with the life of Christ and the dangerous freedom that comes with it? In him, we have the high calling of participating in the redemption of the cosmos. This calling requires that we be activists in the dynamics of every day life. The life we are given in Christ does not flourish when it is hermitized or "protected" from the potential sinning that the freedom of will allows.

The life of liberty flourishes when it meets the chaos of the cosmos head on. In these encounters our faith is truly tested—and it grows stronger. When we face situations we don't know how to handle, we can do as Paul taught: "Walk by the Spirit, and you will not carry out the desire of the flesh" (Gal. 5:16). Our freedom in Christ doesn't shield us from all the normal troubles and pains of our world. But we can live free from their control and free of our past failures. We have the freedom to live as Christ lived.

The position found in Christ

Ephesians: You are accepted Paul begins by reminding us that the most basic position we have is "in Christ." When it comes to knowing what we are going to do with God, we must remember that everything flows out of our primary position of being "in him." Believers are the church of Jesus Christ and, as such, their position is complete acceptance with God. At the beginning of his letter, Paul lets all believers

> "Just because we are accepted does not also entitle us to be autonomous."

know that their acceptability-in-Christ brings with it several important possessions:

- Blessed with every spiritual blessing in Christ (1:3);
- Chosen by him (1:4);
- Complete redemption in him (1:7);
- Knowing his will (1:9);
- Having an inheritance (1:11);
- Being sealed with the Spirit, in him (1:13).

We have these things not just as individuals, but as the church of Jesus Christ. Just because we are accepted does not also entitle us to be autonomous. Our acceptance in Christ defines us as being the body of Christ throughout the world. We are the temples of Christ, and we serve his purposes in the earth, fitted together with other believers to accomplish his will. We have a new self, created in holiness and righteousness. We have been given the nature of Christ so that we share his mission for the redemption of the cosmos.

We are the bride of Christ, called to walk in fidelity and passion with him as we give birth to his purposes in the world. And we are the soldiers of Christ in the world, engaged in actual spiritual conflicts. The outcome of these daily battles determines the progress of God's plan for redemption.

Philippians: You are activated Paul wrote this letter from a prison cell, where he was being held for preaching Christ. His earthly position showed him that he was a captive in jail, but his heavenly position revealed that he was actually free and activated to accomplish the work of God through his life. He did not see himself as disqualified for service. He was fully activated, regardless of his temporary prison residence.

Paul calls us to have the mind of Christ in all things. We are not to think more highly of ourselves than we should, but to put the needs of others before our own. Before coming to the earth, Jesus had all the power and position of God. But when he came to the earth, he willingly "emptied Himself" (2:7) of his divine privileges and took on the limitations of a mere man. We are to empty ourselves of everything that would keep us from living in agreement with God's purposes.

We also have the confidence of Christ. Jesus was so confident because he had "existed in the form of God" (2:6). Yet while he lived on the earth, Jesus depended on the Father's activity in his life to fulfill his mission. Jesus knew from experience that the Father could be trusted to come through, and this knowledge made him confident. We can have the confidence of God the Son when we know him, when he dwells within us.

We have the strength of Christ and have been made capable of doing everything necessary to carry out our kingdom mission. We can do everything necessary because the unlimited strength of Christ lives in us. We do not stand idly by without purpose, assignment, or responsibility. We have been activated for duty, and he will show us what we are to do.

Colossians: You are accomplished Paul writes to these believers in Colossae that they have been rooted in Christ, and they are being built up in him, firmly established in their identity. The central focus of this Epistle is "Jesus Christ as the all-in-all of our identity." This makes sense, since the clearest declaration of Jesus' deity comes through in this book: "For in Him all the fullness of Deity dwells in bodily form" (Col. 2:9). Jesus is the eternal God-man.

> We don't understand that the root of our very existence is inextricably linked with Jesus.

We are rooted in Christ because he is the source of everything created in heaven and on the earth. As believers, then, we are grafted into the root of all life, having the inbred knowledge of *what to do with God*. The reason we struggle with what we will do with God is this: We don't understand that the root of our very existence is inextricably linked with Jesus.

1 and 2 Thessalonians: You are acquired We all want to belong to something bigger than ourselves. In Christ, we have been spoken for; we have been acquired by his death and resurrection. In these two letters, Paul describes three practical ways our position in Christ impacts the way we live:

- *Worthy walk:* Our position in Christ places on us a higher standard of behavior than the rest of the world is allowed.
- *Worthy work*: We are called to expand the kingdom of Christ in the world.
- *Worthy welcome*: When Christ returns in the clouds, he needs to find our lives worthy of his coming.

1 and 2 Timothy: You are appointed Paul appointed Timothy as a pastor, even while Timothy was quite young. These books encourage Timothy to fulfill his calling faithfully. We all have different appointments to fulfill, but the same words of encouragement and instruction that come to Timothy apply to us as well. We may serve in the business world, or in academia, or in the family. Paul encourages us to fulfill our kingdom roles wherever we are.

He also gives us a list of pointed imperatives to help us:

Flee (1 Tim. 6:11);
Pursue (1 Tim. 6:11);
Hold fast (1 Tim. 6:12);
Stir up (2 Tim. 1:6 NIV);

Do not be ashamed (2 Tim. 1:8);
Be aware (2 Tim. 1:15);
Be strong (2 Tim. 2:1);
Be diligent (2 Tim. 2:15);
Avoid (2 Tim. 3:5);
Endure hardship (2 Tim. 4:5).

When hearing these strong words spoken into our situation, we can move forward with increased desire to fulfill our appointment. Speak them to yourself when you're tempted to lighten up on fulfilling your appointment.

Titus: You are altered Our position in Christ has altered us; we'll never be the same. Through his death and resurrection, Jesus forever altered the order of the cosmos. Our position in him brings this new cosmic order to live inside us! In Christ, we become citizens of this new order. Our identity lies in this kingdom of God.

Titus was in charge of selecting new leadership for a church. He had to know how to deal with all ages of people, from all aspects of life. Paul's central word to Titus was for him to do the altering—the influencing—not the other way around.

In Christ, we have become change agents in our world. We are shareholders in the way our world will look. Through our presence the world will receive the opportunity to become the kingdom of God.

Philemon: You are acquitted The slave Onesimus had gone AWOL from his duties to the household of Philemon. He had run off to be with Paul, whom he loved. Paul accepted him for a time, allowing him to serve him even while Paul was in prison. After a time, Paul sent Onesimus back to Philemon with this letter. In the Book of Philemon, Paul asks the slave-owner to forgive and receive back Onesimus *as more than a slave,* but also as a brother in Christ. Paul asked Philemon to acquit Onesimus for any wrong he had committed. He asked Philemon to cancel the debt.

> ❝ We are declared debt free, but we grow into this reality gradually, day by day, as the Spirit works within us. ❞

Christ went to the cross in our place. Our position in him has acquitted us of our personal sin liability and cancelled our debt to pure justice. Instead, we live by God's mercy, in gratitude, seeking to please him. We are no longer responsible to pay our own liability for sin; it has been paid in full. As acquitted people, we tell others how they, too, can have their sin-debt cancelled.

We are declared debt free, but we grow into this reality gradually, day by day, as the Spirit works within us. As we come to realize the depth of our own sin, the full measure of our position in Christ takes on a more complete meaning. And we are able to apply the liberty of our canceled debt to new areas of our lives. We begin to spread out the acquittal we have in Christ to the areas of our lives that need it the most. This is what it means to grow in Christ.

The practical features of faith

These final eight Epistles weren't written by Paul, but by other leaders who bring various perspectives to the practical features of our faith. When viewed as a group, these books provide a depth and richness to all that has already flowed from the Gospels and the Pauline letters.

Hebrews: cultivates faith The writer of Hebrews answers the question "What is faith?" by first showing how inadequate and incomplete the Old Testament sacrifices were. The priests used imperfect lambs to produce finite results. In contrast, Jesus the Son offered himself (as both the perfect high priest and the perfect lamb!). This was a once-for-all sacrifice, with an eternal result (whereas the old system required sacrifice after sacrifice, year after year).

The Book of Hebrews also shows how the lives of Old Testament heroes served as our examples of practical Christian living. Moses, Joshua, Melchizedek, Aaron, and others picture persevering faith in the toughest times.

> 66 Faith is not being completely secure in facts, logic, or verifiable evidence. Faith is being certain about something that is impossible to see! 99

Our heroes of faith accomplished extraordinary things by linking their lives to the powerhouse of God through simple faith. They chose to take God at his word and trust him. After all, faith is not being completely secure in facts, logic, or verifiable evidence. Faith is being certain about something that is impossible to see! It is choosing to take God at his Word. This is possible only as we become more and more intimate with God, proving his faithfulness again and again. Thus we begin to see the invisible with the eyes of God.

James: clearly focused This letter by James shows us what faith does: When it is genuine, it *works*. He gives several examples of what practical faith looks like. A genuine faith affects our behavior; it controls our actions. If someone says they have faith, but it is only a mental attitude without deeds, it could hardly be a genuine faith in Christ. "Faith without works is dead," says James (2:26). Faith that has saved us then focuses our lives on good works.

Real faith is active, it stands up and looks temptation in the face without backing down. It shows no prejudice. It is kind and responsive to the needs of others. It speaks blessings rather than cursing. It spreads peace in the place of strife, and it teaches patience and prayer. Obviously, if we truly have Christ dwelling within us, our outward actions will show it.

1 and 2 Peter: courageous in facing trials So many people identify with Peter! Maybe it's because we tend to overstate what we will do when the chips are down. Peter did just that, saying: "I'll never deny you, Jesus!" But on the day Jesus was taken prisoner he did just what he said he would never do. Three times, when it could cost him his life, Peter succumbed to fear and claimed he never knew Jesus. Later Peter ran away and wept bitterly.

But Peter experienced redemption. He realized that he

was already forgiven, and he returned to do what Jesus taught us all to do: to strengthen the faith of our brothers and sisters in Christ.

These two letters of Peter center on the fiery trials that affect our faith. Christ suffered, and therefore we will suffer. It is to be expected—but so is the ability to stand firm in the midst of the struggle.

1, 2, and 3 John: chooses favor Faith believes the unseen as an already existing reality. It creates in advance the environment to receive the favor of God. Faith creates an environment of love, because, as John stresses: "God is love" (1 John 4:8). In turn, if we do not have love for each other as God loves us, how can we say that we have chosen favor?

We live out love by obeying God. Our obedience rests on a relationship that guides everything about us. The practical side of faith is that it chooses to live in favor with God and with man. Real faith seeks redemption, healing, and restitution. Real faith make the conscious choice of favor.

Jude: celebrates fidelity Many things in life threaten our faith. Jude addresses this and encourages us to guard our faith by testing it, stretching it, and growing it. In other words, if we are to have a strong faith we must exercise it. And our world provides plenty of opportunities to exercise faith!

The New Testament church began to grow and expand more quickly than anyone could have imagined. Most of the leaders continued to grapple with what the church was and how to address its day-to-day ministry needs. They wondered: What is expected of us? How are we to live in the world, and how are we to accomplish God's goals for us?

Even though these letters were written to help the first-century Christians know what to do with God and his plan, they also speak powerfully to us. Why? Because we still struggle with the details of God's ongoing plan to redeem the world. These letters not only show us what *God* is up to, they also show us what *we* can do with the agenda he has for this world.

Our life in Christ is a concrete reality, and we must discover how to flesh it out in the real world. The challenge for each of us is to decide how the life of Christ will look in our lives. Our attitudes and choices will ultimately be revealed in our actions. It is our actions that reveal what we are doing with God and what he is doing with us.

Chapter Eight

HAVE YOU LEFT ME?

Running is a popular form of exercise around the world. Every day thousands of people run mile after mile on trails winding their way through parks and subdivisions. Others run alongside the cars speeding their way down the highways of our land.

I have my own succinct philosophy about running. It contains the words "start slowly" and "taper off." I usually follow up this bit of wisdom with my favorite, "Why run when you can drive?" Each year in my home town, as in many cities around the country, we have several large marathons. They also advertise a "Fun Run."

A fun run. These are two words that should never be found next to each other.

And why do runners wear such crazy clothes? Just look at some of the shorts they wear. I can't tell if their shorts are too short or their legs are too long. And just in case the shorts aren't short enough, they're cut all the way up to the elastic waistband. And how about their shoes? Runners have more different pairs of running shoes than most people have dress shoes. They have running shoes for rain, shoes for sunshine, and shoes for snow. But have you noticed how unhealthy many runners look? Most serious runners have just enough skin stretched over their bones to keep Dr. Kevorkian from calling to set up an appointment.

One saying I always hear about running is "No pain, no gain." I say, "No pain, no pain! That's a good thing." Runners also have a saying that after you run so far you "hit a wall" and everything seems like it's going to implode. This is exactly where the apostle John and the new Christians were. Their numbers and influence in society had grown so quickly that now it felt as if they'd hit a wall. Everything seemed to be ready to implode. Their real question for God was: "Have you left me?"

The first to persecute these new believers were certain powers in the Israelite religious system. Those heading this organized religion saw new believers winning the masses. They could see their own influence eroding before their eyes. Their plans of resistance included persecution.

Rome, too, had it own reasons for persecuting these new believers. Most Romans saw themselves and their society as infinitely superior to this growing group of Christ-followers. They approached this situation the same way they approached most problems: they would bully these "fanatics" out of existence.

The persecution these first-century believers faced was nothing less than that faced by any of Jesus' disciples. For example, tradition holds that the original apostles died in the following ways:

- Matthew suffered martyrdom by being slain with a sword in a city of Ethiopia.
- Mark expired at Alexandria, after being cruelly dragged through the streets.
- Luke was hanged on an olive tree in Greece.
- John was put in a caldron of boiling oil, but escaped death miraculously before he was banished to Patmos.
- Peter was crucified, upside down at Rome.
- James, the Greater, was beheaded at Jerusalem.
- James, the Less, was thrown from a pinnacle of the temple, and then beaten to death with a club.
- Bartholomew was skinned while still alive.
- Andrew was bound to a cross, and preached to his persecutors until he died.
- Thomas was run through the body with a lance in the East Indies.
- Jude was shot to death with arrows.
- Matthias was first stoned and then beheaded.

When Rome burned for six days, Nero blamed the Christians for the fires. Historian Tacitus wrote that Nero arrested Christians and dressed them in wild animal skins to be torn to pieces by dogs. Or he'd crucify them, often covering them in pitch and lighting them on fire. That way they'd serve as human torches to light the night.

Christians threatened anyone in control. But the real reason behind the persecution was *spiritual warfare.* Satan launched into full action trying to discourage and defeat all who would move ahead with Christ. The result was that

> **❝The point of the Book of Revelation is not that you won't be left behind, but that you won't be left alone.❞**

believers everywhere began to ask: "God, have you forgotten me?"

The point of the Book of Revelation is not that you won't be left behind, but that you won't be left alone. Jesus' last words on earth were, "I will always be with you." But in those days of persecution, it didn't feel as if Jesus was with them; they felt abandoned. "Have you left me?" was their cry. "No, you're not alone" was his answer. John receives Jesus' answer in three unforgettable encounters with the living Son of God.

Assured him of his person

I turned to see the voice that was speaking with me. And having turned I saw seven golden lampstands; and in the middle of the lampstands I saw one like a son of man, clothed in a robe reaching to the feet, and girded across His chest with a golden sash. His head and His hair were white like white wool, like snow; and His eyes were like a flame of fire; and His feet were like burnished bronze, when it has been made to glow in a furnace, and His voice was like the sound of many waters.

—Revelation 1:12–15

John describes Jesus just as he saw him. The point Jesus makes by presenting himself to John in these ways is:

"Remember that I am God, and I have not forgotten you." These items make the presentation powerful and memorable—

The robe "These are the garments which they shall make: a breastpiece and an ephod and a robe" (Exod. 28:4). The breastpiece, the ephod, and the robe are the garments of the high priest of the Hebrew faith. The high priest was the only one who could approach God with the sin offering for the people. He put on these specially made garments, covering his entire body, to make himself presentable before God.

In the Book of Hebrews, Jesus is declared to be our Great High Priest, in whom we have full access to God at all times. By appearing to John in the priestly garments of the robe, Jesus is saying that he was present with his people and present with God the Father. The persecuted believers were not left alone.

The hair "I kept looking until thrones were set up, and the Ancient of Days took His seat; His vesture was like white snow and the hair of His head like pure wool. His throne was ablaze with flames, its wheels were a burning fire" (Dan. 7:9). Daniel had many visions and was the interpreter of dreams and visions. In this vision, he saw God sitting on his throne. One of the names for God in the Old Testament is the Ancient of Days. The clothing God wore was as brilliant as untouched snow under an uncovered sun. His hair shone white and soft as pure, combed wool.

John knew Daniel's visions written in the biblical scrolls. It must have struck John that his own vision showed him Jesus as the Son of Man, but also as the Ancient of Days sitting on the throne of eternity. John instantly knew that the One who had *walked* with them on the earth was the same as the One who had *created* the earth. This Jesus now was declaring to all believers that they may have been left behind, but they were not left alone. Jesus had returned to heaven from where he had come, but he was still ever present with all the believers.

The eyes "His body also was like beryl, his face had the appearance of lightning, his eyes were like flaming torches" (Dan. 10:6). In another of his visions, Daniel sees a messenger from God who has come in response to his prayers. The body of this messenger resembles beryl, a precious stone of sea-green color. His face was as brilliant and captivating as a bolt of lightening, and his eyes acted as a flaming torch in a dark room.

In this revelation, John no doubt recognized Jesus for who he had been while he and the other disciples walked with him. Jesus was the ultimate messenger of God who had come to deliver people from the sin holding them captive. In this same element of the vision, Jesus was letting the believers know that he would return to them. He had left them behind, but never alone.

The feet "Feet like the gleam of polished bronze" (Dan. 10:6). Daniel and Ezekiel both saw feet that glowed like bronze. The feet represent the foundation of character in these visions. God's character is stable, immovable, and brilliant, like polished bronze. The character of God is strong and steadfast, capable of supporting everything he has begun and fully capable of subduing all of his enemies, treading them under his feet. Jesus revealed himself as the God of the Old Testament, full of steadfast character and strength. In this way he conveyed to believers that they would never be forgotten.

The voice "I also heard the sound of their wings like the sound of abundant waters as they went, like the voice of the Almighty, a sound of tumult like the sound of an army camp" (Ezek. 1:24). John sat in exile on an island, listening to the overpowering sound of the ocean. The pounding of the surf on a beach can overwhelm even the strongest voice. This is the sound Ezekiel heard again in 43:2, "His voice was like the sound of many waters."

When God speaks, his voice is unmistakable and unavoidable; it demands to be heeded. John heard the voice of God himself, and it came from the mouth of the One he had spent three years with: Jesus Christ. The message for the believers was that even though it seemed everyone spoke against them, God himself would speak on their behalf. They would have to face the indignity of persecution. But they were not forgotten. He remembered everyone of them and would claim them when the time came.

> ❝ The message for the believers was that even though it seemed everyone spoke against them, God himself would speak on their behalf. ❞

The seven stars "He who made the Pleiades and Orion and who changes the darkness into morning ... the LORD is His name" (Amos 5:8). The seven stars is a configuration called Pleiades, a part of the Taurus configuration. Throughout ancient Middle Eastern history, these seven stars symbolized authority and power. Mythology had it that those seven stars were the daughters of Atlas, placed in the heavens by Zeus.

In his day, Caesar declared he held the seven stars. Yet in the revelation of Jesus to John, it is Jesus who holds these stars. He alone possess the power and authority of all creation, and he is the one who made them. Jesus appears to John and the believers as the Creator and possessor of ultimate authority and all power. He reminds them that they are not forgotten, but held in his mighty hand.

Astonished by his performance

Out of His mouth came a sharp two-edged sword.

—Revelation 1:16

The sword was both a defensive and an offensive weapon. In the hand of a master swordsman, it meant sure death to anyone who dared attack. Jesus didn't hold this sword, though. It came out of his mouth, indicating that his words were a sharp and dangerous power. Give heed!

This sword had two edges, polished and sharpened to cut. One side of the blade represented Jesus' words sent out to save and win back the cosmos to himself. The other side represented words spoken to judge Satan and his followers, those who supported and promoted plans against God's plan. The words of Jesus, as a sharp weapon, would cut the bonds holding people in the grasp of heaven's enemies. Jesus' words would also speak the final judgment upon those who had attempted to enslave the cosmos in sin and death.

"When I saw Him, I fell at His feet … . And He placed His right hand on me, saying, 'Do not be afraid, I am the first and the last, and the living One; and I was dead, and behold, I am alive forevermore, and I have the keys of death and of Hades" (Rev. 1:17-18). John was overwhelmed by the revelation he saw. The significance of each of the reported elements was more than he could bear. He was so overcome with the reality of who stood before him that he passed out at the feet of Jesus.

Jesus said he was the first and the last, and the forever living one. Jesus was born as a baby, lived as a man, and died the same human death we all will. Yet his life was perfect, his death was a substitute for us all, and it was followed by the resurrection back to life. He ascended to heaven to provide the only way anyone can ever come back to God. It is Jesus who holds the keys to the kingdom of death and hell. No one dies without his permission, and he makes certain that everyone has the opportunity to be reunited to God through himself.

Affirmed by his presence

John had been on the island, separated from his friends and family, for quite some time. Memories of his days with Jesus washed over him. He put his visions and thoughts on paper so they could be smuggled back to the believers at considerable risk to his visitors.

John knew the encouragement of Jesus. He was exiled, but he was most definitely not alone. John wrote what he had seen to the believers to give them the same affirmation: They were not forgotten or left alone. The God who had led their forefathers out of Egypt was still the God who would lead them through the dark times of present and future oppression.

•••

The Bible begins with four simple words, "In the beginning God." And here in Revelation, it concludes with God revealing himself as one in the same as Jesus Christ. In this vision Jesus is High Priest, the Ancient of Days, the Messenger of God, the established and ruling King, the Voice that all will obey, and the All-Powerful One. This

> **He has never stopped seeking our redemption.**

revelation ties together the entire Scripture into one seamless theme of God's purpose to redeem the cosmos. God has always been pursuing us. He has never stopped seeking our redemption.

When all of our questions have been asked, the one answer that stands the test of time is Jesus Christ. Just as he stood before John and revealed himself as the only adequate resource, he stands before us and our questions, ready to reveal himself as the only satisfactory solution.

He stands ready to reveal to us everything we need to know in order to live life in fidelity with God. Do you know that he's there? Will you trust him? Can you hear him? Do you see him? What are you going to do with him?

He will always be with you.

> *"I am with you always!"*
> *—Matthew 28:20*

READERS' GUIDE

*For Personal Reflection
or Group Discussion*

INTRODUCTION TO
THE READERS' GUIDE

The Questions for Life series gets to the heart of what we believe. Sometimes it's hard to believe that God sticks with us even when we don't deserve it. *Has God Given Up on Me?* is a question that many of us wonder at some point in life. As you read through this book, use the discussion points in the following pages to take you to another level. You can study these points on your own or invite a friend or a group of friends to work through the book with you.

Whether you are just checking God out or desiring to go deeper in your relationship with him, let yourself be challenged to change the way you live based on the answers you discover to life's most pressing questions.

Chapter 1: What's the deal with the Bible?

1. Why is retelling the story of God so important? When have you been able to do this with good result?

2. How is an active view of God different from a static view? Which is your own view?

3. What amazes you the most about the unity of the Bible? Have you considered how important its unity is?

4. What is the continuing message of the Bible today? What impact does it have upon your own attitudes and actions?

5. In what ways would you like the Bible to become more a part of your everyday life? How can your group members pray for you in this regard?

Chapter 2: Do you know I'm here?

1. Why do you think we elevate people to near-perfect status?

2. In what ways did God provide life through Genesis?

3. In what areas of your life have you seen God's deliverance? How would you express your gratitude right now?

4. Why are we so prone to go back to the bondage we've been freed from? What works best when trying to get out of such slavery?

5. Throughout the first five books of the Bible, God gives reminders. What sticks out most to you about these reminders? Which ones do you, personally, need the most?

Chapter 3: Will you trust me?

1. God told Joshua that if he trusted, then he'd spend time in the Bible. Have you demonstrated your trust in God by spending time in his Word?

2. What is the inherent shortfall of looking for external situations to change?

3. How is the hand of God made active in our lives?

4. What do you struggle with most concerning change? What advice would you offer to a friend with similar struggles?

5. What do you face that makes it hard for you to trust God these days?

Chapter 4: Do you hear me?

1. What things make it hard for us to hear from God in the midst of disorder?

2. What kind of approach to God does Psalm 22 show us?

3. How does knowing the character of God impact our choices? Talk about a time when this was true in your own choice.

4. Why is it so hard for people to hear from God while trying to figure out their lives? What has this been like for you?

5. When have you experienced the intimacy with God that is described in the Song of Songs?

Chapter 5: Do you see it?

1. What traps do we find ourselves in that cause us to part ways with God?

2. In what ways do we avoid taking responsibility for our wrong actions? If you are in such a situation now, consider how you might put an end to that avoidance.

3. From Daniel, what do we learn about the participation of
   God?

4. What hope does the theme of Jonah give you?

5. What is the central message of the prophets? Has this chapter
   helped you see the common thread in the prophets?

6. What one theme from the prophets would you like to apply
   to your life? Why?

Chapter 6: Where is the love?

1. What does Mark teach about the person of Jesus? How had
   the Jews missed it?

2. What are some ways we are like the Romans as we search for
   love?

3. In what ways does Luke show Jesus meeting the needs of people?

4. Which miracle best addresses a way in which you need to
   experience Jesus?

5. Which of the seven encounters revealed Jesus in a meaningful way to you? Why?

Chapter 7: What am I going to do with you?

1. What are some of the transitions that took place in the Book of Acts?

2. Name some reasons people choose legalism over freedom. When have you done so? Do you recommend it?

3. From the first division of the Epistles, which principle do you need to apply to your life? What hindrances may keep you from doing this?

4. How does knowing your position in Christ help you in your walk? What have you learned from knowing who you are in Christ?

5. In your opinion, do most people view their faith as being practical? How does the last division of the Epistles illustrate the practical application of your faith? What does this mean for you?

Chapter 8: Have you left me?

1. What is the underlying theme of the Book of Revelation? How is this different from what you may have previously thought?

2. What are the reasons that we, like the early Christians, feel as if we have been left alone? Have you been there?

3. What have you learned about the person of Jesus from his description in the Book of Revelation?

4. What does Jesus' sword practically mean for us today?

5. What words of praise and worship would you like to offer to Jesus right now?

The Word at Work Around the World

A vital part of Cook Communications Ministries is our international outreach, Cook Communications Ministries International (CCMI). Your purchase of this book, and of other books and Christian-growth products from Cook, enables CCMI to provide Bibles and Christian literature to people in more than 150 languages in 65 countries.

Cook Communications Ministries is a not-for-profit, self-supporting organization. Revenues from sales of our books, Bible curricula, and other church and home products not only fund our U.S. ministry, but also fund our CCMI ministry around the world. One hundred percent of donations to CCMI go to our international literature programs.

CCMI reaches out internationally in three ways:

· Our premier International Christian Publishing Institute (ICPI) trains leaders from nationally led publishing houses around the world.

· We provide literature for pastors, evangelists, and Christian workers in their national language.

· We reach people at risk—refugees, AIDS victims, street children, and famine victims—with God's Word.

Word Power, God's Power

Faith Kidz, RiverOak, Honor, Life Journey, Victor, NexGen — every time you purchase a book produced by Cook Communications Ministries, you not only meet a vital personal need in your life or in the life of someone you love, but you're also a part of ministering to José in Colombia, Humberto in Chile, Gousa in India, or Lidiane in Brazil. You help make it possible for a pastor in China, a child in Peru, or a mother in West Africa to enjoy a life-changing book. And because you helped, children and adults around the world are learning God's Word and walking in his ways.

Thank you for your partnership in helping to disciple the world. May God bless you with the power of his Word in your life.

For more information about our international ministries, visit www.ccmi.org.

Additional copies of *Has God Given Up on Me?*
and other NexGen titles are available
from your local bookseller.
Look for the other books in the Questions for Life series:

Why Is it Taking Me so Long to Be Better?
What Happens When I Die?
Did I Get Out of Bed for This?
How Safe Am I?
Why Is This Happening to Me?

If you have enjoyed this book,
or if it has had an impact on your life,
we would like to hear from you.

Please contact us at:

NEXGEN BOOKS
Cook Communications Ministries, Dept. 201
4050 Lee Vance View
Colorado Springs, CO 80918
Or visit our Web site: www.cookministries.com

NE✗GEN®

Building the New Generation of Believers